21
Things God
Never Said

21
Things God
Never Said

*Correcting Our Misconceptions
About Evangelism*

R. Larry Moyer

21 Things God Never Said: Correcting Our Misconceptions About Evangelism

© 2004 by R. Larry Moyer

Published by Kregel Publications, a division of Kregel, Inc., P.O. Box 2607, Grand Rapids, MI 49501.

Cover design: John M. Lucas

Library of Congress Cataloging-in-Publication Data
Moyer, R. Larry.
  21 things God never said: correcting our misconceptions about evangelism / by R. Larry Moyer.
    p. cm.
Includes bibliographical references.
  1. Evangelistic work. 2. Witness bearing(Christianity).
I. Title: Twenty-one things God never said. II. Title.
BV3790.M8355   2004
269'.2—dc22   2004013234

ISBN 0-8254-3171-9

Printed in the United States of America

06 07 08 / 5 4 3 2

To
Dr. Haddon W. Robinson,
in appreciation for his impact on my
life. Through his help, I learned grace
and the need to carefully study
the Scriptures.

Contents

((•))

Contents

Contents

Introduction

((•))

God never meant evangelism to be a pain. He meant it to be a privilege. It's to be a delight, not a dread.

Unfortunately, evangelism isn't always seen by believers as the privilege it is. One reason for this is that some people make statements about evangelism as though they're speaking the "gospel truth," when in fact they're promoting myths. These misconceptions have decreased clarity in presenting the gospel.

Paul admonished Timothy to rightly divide the word of truth (2 Tim. 2:15), and God begs the same of us. When it comes to evangelism and salvation, though, some believers too often use verses out of context. As a result, other believers feel guilty about their lack of evangelistic efforts or are motivated to evangelize out of fear and shame, motivational tools God does not use.

A correct and biblical approach to evangelism enhances clarity. *21 Things God Never Said* corrects many misconceptions, so the message that is clear in God's mind becomes clear in ours. Believers also begin to understand how God has given us an undeserved privilege—the privilege of making a difference in where people spend eternity. With that understanding, believers can then evangelize in the same way they are saved—out of grace, not guilt.

May God use this book to help you approach evangelism from a biblical perspective. May it excite you about what excites the heart of God—reaching the lost for Christ!

"If you don't know the date you were saved, then you're not saved."

$((\bullet))$

The fall breeze blowing through the windows of the Michigan farmhouse was refreshing. The conversation was warm. Sitting across the room from me, the husband talked about the day he was saved, the day an exciting transformation took place in his life. His wife, though, appeared uneasy. They were both clear on the only means of salvation—trusting Christ alone to save you. So why was one uneasy and the other so excited?

The thought struck me, *Is she uncomfortable because she can't tell me the exact date she met the Savior?* So I volunteered, "The exciting thing is, as long as you're trusting Christ alone, you're saved—regardless of when you crossed the line. You don't have to know the exact date it happened."

Her eyes brightened. "That's my problem," she said. "I understand the salvation message and know I've trusted Christ, but I just can't tell you what day it happened. I was so afraid you were going to ask the exact date I was saved. For me, it was more gradual until one day I realized that I could tell people that I was saved."

As a spiritually searching teen, I too heard that mistaken emphasis on a date. I'm sad to say that it came from an evangelist. With an authoritative voice he warned, "If you don't know the day you were saved, you're not saved." I now know that he didn't mean you had to give the exact date, such as October 16. He meant there had to be an actual day in your mind—one you could look back to and say, "I vividly remember—on that day I was saved."

At the time, though, I felt torn. Should I go through the motions of coming to Christ again? That seemed foolish when I'd already done so. Yet if I wasn't sure of the date, would I get in trouble with God because He demands something I couldn't give? I felt confused, frustrated, and scared.

How does the emphasis on a specific date hinder us in evangelism? First, doubt about salvation takes away the freedom and joy of speaking about Christ. How can we speak of the ecstasy of heaven if there's *any* question we'll be there ourselves? When I first trusted Christ, I wanted everyone to know heaven could be theirs. But I wondered, *Can I tell them how to be saved if I can't give the exact date of my salvation?* I felt like my foot was on the brake and the gas pedal at the same time. I wanted to go forward but couldn't.

Second, the emphasis on a date hinders our approach to certain people. What do we say to those who declare they're saved yet can't give an exact date when they "crossed the line"?

What do Scriptures emphasize?

What's the problem with that statement the evangelist made when I was a teen? Scripture never makes such a statement.

The Gospel of John explains how to receive eternal life. Read the following passages and note the number of times they mention anything about knowing the date you were saved.

Whoever believes in Him should not perish but have eternal life. (John 3:15)

For God so loved the world that He gave His only begotten Son, that whoever believes in Him should not perish but have everlasting life. (John 3:16)

He who believes in Him is not condemned; but he who does not believe is condemned already, because he has not believed in the name of the only begotten Son of God. (John 3:18)

He who believes in the Son has everlasting life; and he who does not believe the Son shall not see life, but the wrath of God abides on him. (John 3:36)

Most assuredly, I say to you, he who hears My word and believes in Him who sent Me has everlasting life, and shall not come into judgment, but has passed from death into life. (John 5:24)

And Jesus said to them, "I am the bread of life. He who comes to Me shall never hunger, and he who believes in Me shall never thirst." (John 6:35)

And this is the will of Him who sent Me, that everyone who sees the Son and believes in Him may have everlasting life; and I will raise him up at the last day. (John 6:40)

Most assuredly, I say to you, he who believes in Me has everlasting life. (John 6:47)

I am the resurrection and the life. He who believes in Me, though he may die, he shall live. And whoever lives and believes in Me shall never die. Do you believe this? (John 11:25–26)

But these are written that you may believe that Jesus is the Christ, the Son of God, and that believing you may have life in His name. (John 20:31)

How many times did these verses mention knowing the date you were saved? If you said zero, you're right. When Scripture gives assurance of salvation, it goes back to a *fact,* not a date. The real question is,

"Who am I trusting in right now?" If we're trusting Christ alone to save us, we're saved regardless of when and where we crossed the line. Our salvation is established by *Who* we place our trust in, not *when* we trusted Him.

Did a particular day of salvation exist?

Is becoming a child of God something that happened at a point of time, or is it a process? Yes, there was that instant in which He "delivered us from the power of darkness and conveyed us into the kingdom of the Son of His love" (Col. 1:13). But coming to understand the message of salvation may have occurred over days, weeks, months, or even years. Although the actual *transition* from Satan's kingdom to God's kingdom happened in a second, having to know the date that transition occurred is not taught in Scripture.

It's true that in Scripture, some new converts spoke of the specific moment when they met the Savior. Paul's conversion, for example, is found in Acts 9. He recounted that conversion in Acts 22 and again in Acts 26. The day he met the Savior was clear in his mind. Even the hour was clear—around noon. He spoke of the dramatic experience, highlighting details of a blinding light and thunderous voice from heaven, falling to the ground, and his own response to the Lord.

The Ethiopian eunuch certainly could have given us details about the day he met the Savior. We can read the actual details in Acts 8:26–39, but it's easy to imagine what he would have told his friends. "I was returning from worship in Jerusalem and reading from the prophet Isaiah, when all of a sudden . . ." No doubt he would have mentioned meeting Philip and coming to understand that Christ is, indeed, the Son of God. He probably would have been as specific about the day of his conversion as Paul was about his. Upon trusting Christ the Ethiopian was baptized and then saw Philip supernaturally vanish.

The appearance and then sudden disappearance of the one who led a person to the Savior would have etched that day in any person's mind. How could anyone *not* clearly remember such an extraordinary day? But to say the day we crossed the line from darkness into light must be as vivid in our minds as it was in the mind of Paul or the Ethiopian, mishandles those accounts.

The Bible emphasizes that salvation is a personal decision that no one can make for us. It's also clear that Christ is the only means to salvation. Equally clear is that there is a particular moment when we move from being children of darkness to children of light. We must know Whose we are and why we are His. We must know, too, that through personal trust in Christ alone to save us we have appropriated His death. But we are never told that we must know the precise moment that occurred.

Why the mistaken emphasis on a date?

When evangelizing, we haven't always asked, "Is this what the Bible really teaches?" Too easily, we lay the Bible aside. Statements are made without being examined for biblical truth.

When evangelizing, we meet those who say, "I've always been a Christian." In reality, that means, "I've never *become* a Christian." We're not born Christians; we're born sinners. Sin originates from Adam, so the whole race stands guilty before God. Romans 5:12 tells us, "Therefore, just as through one man sin entered the world, and death through sin, and thus death spread to all men, because all sinned." Wanting to alarm, zealous evangelists have sometimes said, "If you don't know the date you were saved, you're not saved." But it's wrong to make claims that Scripture doesn't, just to make people aware of their sinful condition.

A better approach is, (1) "Are you confident that if you were to die right now you'd go to heaven?" and (2) "If you were to stand before God and He were to ask, 'Why should I let you into heaven?' what would you tell Him?"

The night before my flight to an evangelistic outreach in Pennsylvania, I'd hardly slept. So when the jet engines started humming, my head nodded. Soon, the lull of the plane's motion rocked me to sleep. Two hours later, I awoke and got into a conversation with the man to my right. He noticed that I had a book about spiritual matters and asked, "Are you a preacher?" I responded, "Yes, I am." He unloaded his personal difficulties, and told me that his wife had just left him. He was devastated. We were about to land, so we couldn't talk extensively, but I learned that he was returning to Dallas on Sunday (whereas I would be returning on Monday). I said, "Why don't I give you a call and let's get together to talk. I'd love to help." We exchanged phone numbers and I gave him my copy of the "May I Ask You a Question?" tract (see Appendix).

When I returned to Dallas, I called him and we met for breakfast. It turns out that the man once played professional football with the NFL, which was confirmed by his husky, linebacker appearance. He shared why his wife of seven years was leaving him, and admitted they'd both made mistakes. I listened with compassion then said, "Your marriage may be over but your life isn't. God still wants good things to happen, and He wants to use you." I shared that everything begins with a personal relationship with Christ. So I asked, "Have you come to a point that, if you were to die, you know you'd go to heaven?" He answered, "Yes."

At this point, some would have asked, "Exactly when did you come to Christ?" I know he couldn't have told me, and I'd already determined that he didn't understand the gospel. So I asked, "If you stood before God and He were to ask you, 'Why should I let you into heaven?' what would you tell him?" He explained that he'd tried to do what was right and lived a good life. I responded, "What would you say if I told you that God wouldn't accept that answer?" He was surprised. I went through my Bad News/Good News presentation of the gospel (see Appendix), explaining that eternal life is a free gift. He was overwhelmed with what he was seeing in Scripture. Over pancakes and sausage, we prayed together, and he told God that he was trusting Christ to save him—and he told me how grateful he was that God had placed him next to me on the plane. We agreed to get together again so I could begin discipling him.

Some know the date, some don't.

The reason many people *do* know the precise moment they were saved is because their conversion was dramatic. It may have been preceded by the loss of a mate or a job, or the sudden news of a terminal disease. It may have been in conjunction with a debilitating accident or addiction to a particular substance. Severe depression leading to thoughts of suicide may have shown some people their spiritual need.

While speaking at a church in Illinois, I talked with one believer there and asked, "When did you come to know the Lord?" His face lit up. Beaming from ear to ear he responded, "March 16, 1991, 9:45 P.M." When I heard the details of his conversion, I understood why the specific moment was so vivid to him.

On that date, the young man had been riding in a car with a fellow student. She was excited about her faith and wanted to share it. Since there was little traffic on the four-lane highway, the young woman engaged him in conversation. She said, "If you could ask God anything, what would you ask Him?" He shocked her by breaking down in tears, confessing he was far from God. Involved in a homosexual lifestyle, he thought God wouldn't want anything to do with him. Explaining the gospel, she led him to Christ. Because the young man had wrecked his life, tears preceded his conversion. It's doubtful that he'll forget the day or circumstances.

Not all conversions, though, are as dramatic. Some people come to Christ from a liberal religious background. The only reason they weren't saved is because no one had ever explained the gospel to them. Then they began attending a Bible-teaching church and learned that Christ saves sinners. As the gospel of grace was proclaimed, they trusted Christ and received eternal life. As they grew in Christ, they thought, *Wait a minute. That means years ago, when I was attending that liberal church I wasn't saved.* When these people give their testimony, they are clear: "I was lost but now I'm found." Sometimes they can't tell you the precise day they were saved. They just know they're saved.

A believer told me, "I can't give you the specific date when I trusted Christ. It was sometime during my first months in college. But I do know Jesus Christ died and rose again for my sake." Stressing that all people have to know the date they were saved ignores the varying backgrounds from which God saves people.

Again, there is a particular instant in which one's eternal destiny is forever changed. But when Scripture gives assurance of salvation, it goes back to a fact, not a date. If you're trusting Christ alone, you're saved regardless of when the divine transaction took place.

Why a fact, not a date?

Why is the fact—not the date—important? First, *Who* saved us results in our security, not *when*. We're saved because we are His regardless of when we became His. We must put the emphasis in the same place God does. Christ affirmed, "He who believes in Me has everlasting life" (John 6:47).

Second, as you give your testimony, *when* you were saved is of little help. No one can come to Christ *when* you did. That moment passed. Each person must come to Christ the way you did—as a sinner trusting Christ. If you know the date, feel free to mention it, but what helps most is relating *how* you were saved—by grace through faith.

A third reason why the fact and not the date is important is that many people, when they see Christ, will discover they only *thought* they knew the exact day of their salvation. The eternal transaction took place a week, or even months, later when they really understood the gospel.

I confess to possibly being one of those people. I came to understand the gospel through my own Bible study while growing up on my dad's dairy farm in Lancaster, Pennsylvania. I plowed the fields, cultivated the corn, and hoed the garden. Perspiration rolled off my face, but I hardly noticed. My thoughts were on what I was learning—eternal life is free. When the truth dawned there on the farm, I dropped to my knees by my bed one night and trusted Christ. Then, when I attended Philadelphia Biblical University and learned more about God's grace and eternal security, I was ecstatic. I grasped the unconditional love of God like never before. I wonder at times, did I really trust Christ that night on the dairy farm? Or was I saved during my first year of Bible college? I look forward to finding out!

A fourth reason to emphasize fact and not date is that stressing a date often confuses others, especially children. Children understand better as they mature. They then question whether they understood the gospel when they thought they came to Christ. They're relieved to know that if they're trusting Christ alone they are saved. The moment salvation occurred is not the issue.

A sensitive, first-year Bible college student once came up to me with tears running down her cheeks. She shared, "You've just relieved me of a tremendous burden. It's now completely gone." She explained that her parents had told her that she came to Christ as a small child, but she wasn't sure that she'd really understood it back then. Her parents kept saying, "All we remember is, you prayed and we're sure that's when you came to Christ." They may have been sure, but she wasn't. Now, understanding that the issue is fact not a date, she said, "I now know I'm saved and I know why." Her doubt could have been avoided had she not been burdened by the mistaken and unbiblical emphasis on date.

Conclusion

If you know the date you were saved, the Savior is exalted. If you don't know the exact day, but know you're trusting Christ alone, the Savior is exalted. Understanding *Who* saved us and *how* we were saved is what matters. Recalling the exact date of our salvation does not.

> **If you trust Christ alone to save you, you are saved. You don't have to know the exact date. It's the Who and the how of our salvation that matters, not the date.**

"If you don't tell others about Me, then you're not a Christian."

$((\bullet))$

Get out your legal pad and your yellow #2 pencil. Or your cross pen. Or your laptop. List what God has done for you, including what He's given you. Make the list extensive. Include tangibles, of course, like food, friends, and furniture, but don't forget intangibles—such as the air you breathe. Set the list aside for a few minutes then return. You'll remember things you've overlooked. It's, in fact, impossible to list *everything* a loving God has given to you.

Now examine that list carefully. Not a single item that you wrote is more important than eternal life. My list includes an understanding wife. Her warmth sustains me during difficult times. My list also includes the friends God has given to me. But the gift of my wife and friends cannot match His gift of salvation. What makes the gift so amazing is that Jesus Christ paid the price when He died in our place on a cross and declared, "It is finished" (John 19:30). Trusting Christ, we are forever accepted by God, not based upon what we've done for Him but based upon what He has done for us. Again, the gift is eternal, and because my wife and close friends have trusted Christ, we're going to live together *forever*.

What could be a better message than the one surrounding that gift? What greater privilege than to be what Acts 1:8 calls "witnesses to Me"? Could the great privilege of sharing that message be one reason that evangelism is *assumed* more than it is asserted in the New Testament? Why *not* share the gospel? Why miss an opportunity?

Some people, though, carry that opportunity a step further by attaching a warning—if you don't tell others about Christ then you're not a Christian. They aren't saying you cease to be a Christian. They mean you never *were* a Christian—you only *thought* you were. They argue, "If you're a Christian, you'd speak to others about Christ."

What are the difficulties about such a declaration?

Four difficulties stand out. First, not a single verse in the Bible makes such a statement. "Whoever believes" is the only condition for receiving eternal life. "Whoever believes *and tells others about Me*" is not a condition for receiving eternal life. One of the best known verses in the Bible, John 3:16, declares, "For God so loved the world that He gave His only begotten Son, that whoever believes in Him should not perish but have everlasting life." That verse doesn't say, "Whoever believes in Him *and tells others about Him.*"

A second difficulty is that, of the numerous conversions recorded in the New Testament, telling others about Christ is never given as a condition of salvation. One remarkable account is the Samaritan woman of John 4. She was convinced that the One to whom she was speaking was the promised Messiah. She "left her waterpot, went her way into the city, and said to the men, 'Come, see a Man who told me all things that I ever did. Could this be the Christ?'" (John 4:28–29). Ten verses later we read, "And many of the Samaritans of that city believed in Him because of the word of the woman who testified, 'He told me all that I ever did'" (v. 39). Her evangelistic effort was the *result* of her grasping that Christ was the promised Messiah. It was not a *condition* of her salvation. Verse 10 of the same chapter established the condition for Christ's saving her. Christ said, "If you knew the gift of God, and who it is who says to you, 'Give Me a drink,' you would have asked Him, and He would have given you living water." Other conversion accounts give the same message. Telling others about Christ is never a condition of salvation; it should be a result of salvation as we grow in His grace.

Common sense tells us the third difficulty. If any condition is attached to a gift, it's no longer free. Suppose a friend said, "I'd like to give you a condo in the mountains. It's yours for life, free, all expenses paid. You owe nothing. The title and documents that make the transfer official have been drawn up. Will you receive this gift?" Of course you're excited, you thank your friend for being so kind, receive the gift, and move in. You bathe your feet in the cool mountain streams. You photograph deer as they browse in nearby meadows. You lie on your back watching the trees clap their limbs together. You sip hot cocoa by the fireplace in the condo at night. After you've lived there a year, the friend asks, "Have you told anyone what I did for you?" You reply, "Well . . . no. I guess I probably should have, but I do appreciate it." The friend then says, "In that case, the mountain condo was never yours." A gift is only a gift if no strings are attached.

A fourth difficulty is critical. If to be a Christian one must tell others about the Savior, we're left with two dilemmas. One is that deathbed conversions would not be possible. That would include the thief on the cross (Luke 23:39–43). If one has to evangelize to be a Christian, time and opportunity are essential. That isn't always possible in a sterile hospital room or on the roadside as the helicopter lands or the ambulance speeds in. Yet I believe there will be many in heaven who, in the final moment of life, trusted Christ. Their weakened condition or solitude may not have allowed opportunity to say His name to another person. The second dilemma is that we'd need two gospels or two ways to salvation. One gospel would be for the person who has time to tell others, and another would be for the person who doesn't. Two separate gospels is not scriptural.

Shouldn't you want someone else to have what you have?

"Wait a minute," you might say. "How can you be a sincere Christian without evangelizing? If one is really saved, doesn't it 'spill over' to someone else?"

Any number of things can hold us back from evangelizing, including fear of rejection. John 12:42 is a good example: "Nevertheless even among the rulers many *believed in Him*, but because of the Pharisees they did not confess Him, lest they should be put out of the synagogue" (emphasis added). "Believed in Him" is a common Johannine expression for saving faith. (In John 8:30 we read, "As He spoke these words, many believed in Him.") These rulers, then, had genuine faith, but they didn't confess Christ. John, here in verse 42, is contrasting the believing rulers to those in verses 37–41 who did not believe. Those mentioned in verse 42 trusted Christ, but they feared being kicked out of the synagogue, so they didn't confess Him publicly.

A woman talked with me about spiritual things. Soon we were on the subject of evangelism. I thought, *What a people person. She's pleasant with her appearance, tone, and words. She could be effective in evangelism.* Then she said, "What I really want to ask is, why am I so afraid to talk to others about Christ? And am I the only one this scared?" I couldn't resist laughing. I told her how normal she was. When I mentioned the word *rejection,* she interrupted. "That's what I'm afraid of. I don't like rejection." Fear of rejection holds us back just as it held back New Testament believers.

The frequency of our witness, then, is not the issue in our salvation. The issue is, Who is the object of our faith? Do we acknowledge that we are sinners? Do we believe that Christ died as our substitute and rose again? And are we willing to trust in Christ alone to save us? If so, we *should* want to tell others about Him. The presence or lack of that witness, though, is never a condition of salvation.

How, then, does evangelism fit?

Telling others about Christ is not a requirement for salvation. It's a requirement for discipleship.

The first thing Christ taught His disciples is found in Matthew 4:19, "Follow Me, and I will make you fishers of men." If they were going to follow, they had to fish—for men. His message was, "I want people who will follow because I want people who will fish." As the disciples followed, He would teach them how.

Becoming a Christian and becoming a disciple are not synonymous.

Becoming a Christian involves receiving His gift. Christ said to the Samaritan woman, "If you knew the gift of God, and who it is who says to you, 'Give Me a drink,' you would have asked Him, and He would have given you living water" (John 4:10). Revelation 22:17 instructs, "Whoever desires, let him take the water of life freely." Then when a person becomes a Christian, God says, "Will you now be my disciple?" Disciple means "learner." Christ warns that following after Him and learning more about Him involves a cost: "If anyone comes to Me and does not hate his father and mother, wife and children, brothers and sisters, yes, and his own life also, he cannot be My disciple. And whoever does not bear his cross and come after Me cannot be My disciple" (Luke 14:26–27).

The best man in my wedding is now a pastor in Indiana. His friendship enriched my wedding ceremony, and it has enriched my life ever since. I appreciate his consistent growth and walk with the Lord. He sincerely cares for lost people. If you ask him why, he'll answer, "Because that's the first thing Christ taught His disciples." He loves the Savior, desires to be a disciple, cares for the lost.

To say that one cannot be a Christian without being involved in evangelism is not biblical. To say that one cannot be a *disciple* without in some way being involved in evangelism *is* biblical.

Conclusion

The Bible does not teach that telling others about Christ is a condition for salvation. Eternal life is a gift. Upon receiving that gift, God invites us to be His disciples. As we follow after Him and learn more about Him, we learn that evangelism is part of discipleship. He wants the first thing on His heart to also be the first thing on ours—the lost.

> **Telling others is one of the first steps of discipleship, not a condition for becoming a Christian.**

Misconception 3

"You shouldn't keep company with sinners."

$((\bullet))$

This crisp September day was tailor-made for golf, thought Doug. And coming up to the eighteenth hole on the green, Doug knew that he couldn't have played better. Nick knew that he couldn't have played worse. Doug was a little surprised that Nick wasn't by now letting a few expletives fly. How many times, after all, had Nick heard Doug let go a string of them? Cursing just seemed to come naturally to Doug.

After the final round, Nick slid alongside Doug in the golf cart and congratulated him with a strong pat on the back. "You're a pro," said Nick, making Doug's day. Nick continued to talk about his game, then after a moment or two of silence, he said, "You know, Doug, I've noticed that you mention Christ a lot when things aren't going your way. I refer to him too, but you may have noticed it's in a different way. Tell me, have you ever thought much about Him? Not just as a word, but as a Person?" Doug was stunned, speechless, maybe even a little embarrassed. No one had ever been quite so direct with him before. It got him to thinking.

Four weeks later, Nick's Savior became Doug's, and he could hardly wait to make one special phone call—to his brother, who he knew had been praying for him for a long time. With the zeal of a new Christian Doug told his brother about Nick and how he came to the decision to trust Christ. His brother was thrilled. They continued the conversation, catching up on work, family, and sports. In the course of conversation,

Doug mentioned his plans for the weekend, which included some activities with his old friends—non-Christian friends. Most of his friends were, after all, non-Christians. Doug was shocked when his brother said, "Now that you're a Christian, you need to drop your old friends. The Bible says you shouldn't keep company with sinners. It's time to find some new friends."

Many new Christians receive that advice. I was in the classroom doing what I love—exciting students about evangelism. I told about some people that I knew—my unbelieving barber, the non-Christian I jog with, and a friend who didn't know the Lord. I shared with excitement about time spent with non-Christians—contacts which often lead to conversions.

I sensed surprise and alarm. Some of the students' faces displayed concern. They glanced at each other as if wondering if they should say something. During a break, one student told me why he and some of the others struggled. "We've been told that, now that we're Christians, we must separate ourselves from unbelievers. But how can we evangelize if we don't have any non-Christian friends?"

Those around us impact us. The right kind of people encourage spiritual growth. The wrong kind can impede our spiritual walk. Those who are concerned for believers—especially for new converts—emphasize, "Now you need a new circle of friends. The Bible teaches that you shouldn't keep company with unbelievers."

How is that a misconception? Isn't Scripture used to support that thought? Yes, but let's examine the two verses most often used to see what they're really saying.

Where does such a thought originate?

1 Corinthians 5:9

In 1 Corinthians 5:9 we're told, "I wrote to you in my epistle not to keep company with sexually immoral people." It might appear that verse discourages contact with non-Christians, especially if they are "sexually immoral." But read ahead one verse where Paul defined who he meant by the "sexually immoral people." He continued, "Yet I certainly did not mean with the sexually immoral people of this world, or with the covetous, or extortioners, or idolaters, since then you would need to go out of the world. But now I have written to you not to keep company with anyone named *a brother,* who is sexually immoral, or covetous, or an idolater, or a reviler, or a drunkard, or an extortioner—not even to eat with such a person" (emphasis added).

Paul was referring to *believers* who are sexually immoral, not unbelievers. He said, "I certainly did not mean with the sexually immoral people of this world." His reasoning is easy to follow. The believers were to discipline those inside the church and let God discipline those outside. He explains, "For what have I to do with judging those also who are outside? Do you not judge those who are inside? But those who are outside God judges. Therefore 'put away from yourselves the evil person'" (1 Cor. 5:12–13).

Paul's admonition is similar to the one he used in 2 Thessalonians 3:14–15: "And if anyone does not obey our word in this epistle, note that person and do not keep company with him, that he may be ashamed. Yet do not count him as an enemy, but admonish him as a brother."

Paul wasn't warning against spending time with unbelievers, he was warning against spending time with disobedient believers. To say that 1 Corinthians 5:9 warns us not to keep company with non-Christians is an abuse of the passage.

James 4:4

In James 4:4 we read, "Adulterers and adulteresses! Do you not know that friendship with the world is enmity with God? Whoever therefore wants to be a friend of the world makes himself an enemy of God." From that verse, it's commonly concluded that to have friendships with non-Christians is to be a friend of the world.

James wrote to believers undergoing severe trials. Sometimes, when we go through trials, we treat worst those whom we know the best. As a result, conflicts arise between believers and their brothers and sisters in the family of God. James began this section by asking, "Where do wars and fights come from among you?" (v. 1).

One source of conflict, James explained, is wrong associations. The believers he wrote about were living closer to the world than to Christ. By "adulterers and adulteresses" he wasn't referring to those committing literal adultery, but to those whose lives weren't always Christlike. Keep in mind, James was writing a general epistle to Christians who were courting the world instead of courting Christ. They acted like the world acted. They thought like the world thought. They did what the world did. In so doing, they were warring against God. James declared, "Whoever therefore wants to be a friend of the world makes himself an enemy of God" (v. 4).

James wasn't forbidding friendship with non-Christians. He was forbidding believers to think, act, and talk like the world. They were to be in the world but not of it. Although residents of the world, they needed to live as citizens of heaven. A ship is safe in the ocean as long as the ocean is not in the ship. Likewise, a Christian is safe in the world as long as the world is not in the Christian. James is telling the believers that they need to think the way Christ thinks, not the way the world thinks.

When we spend time with non-Christians, we must not act and think the way they do. We ought to influence non-Christians, not let them influence us. In no way, though, was James forbidding friendships with non-Christians.

We can't do personal evangelism without personal contact.

When Christ called His disciples, He exhorted, "Follow Me, and I will make you fishers of men" (Matt. 4:19). Fishing for men requires contacting men. Contacting men requires conversing with men. Those conversations may take place in the home or the workplace, across the net of a tennis court, or at the back of a bowling alley. They may take one hour or five hours. They may lead to an invitation to dinner or an invitation to play golf. In the midst of those contacts and conversations, the gospel is shared, and people face their need for Christ.

A Christian friend of mine likes to play tennis. That's normal. What's abnormal is who he likes to play with. When he slams the ball across the net, he prefers a non-Christian opponent. Should the unbeliever become a believer, he finds a new tennis partner. Why? He uses the tennis court to reach people for Christ because he sees the tennis court as his friendship court. Those friendships have allowed him to impact non-Christians. Tennis on the court leads to talking off the court. Talking leads to Christ.

Personal evangelism necessitates personal contact. If Jesus Christ had been opposed to us having relationships with non-Christians, why would He have encouraged us to evangelize?

To be Christlike, we must spend time with non-Christians.

People were upset with Jesus Christ, but not because He spoke to sinners. What disturbed them was that He *spent time* with sinners. In Luke 15:1–2 we are told, "Then all the tax collectors and the sinners drew near to Him to hear Him. And the Pharisees and scribes complained, saying, 'This Man receives sinners and eats with them.'"

Tax collectors were despised because of their occupation. The law allowed them to overtax the people and keep the remainder for themselves. They adhered to the philosophy, "What's mine is mine and what's yours is mine." Sinners were despised because of their lifestyle. For them, standards rarely existed; immorality, deception, and thievery were the norm.

Why would Christ spend time with such a despicable crowd? His explanation was, "I say to you that likewise there will be more joy in heaven over one sinner who repents than over ninety-nine just persons who need no repentance" (Luke 15:7). Jesus Christ was not contrasting a repentant sinner to a sinless saint. Nor was He implying that the shameful behavior of the sinner is more acceptable than the behavior of hypocritical Pharisees, who tried to obey God. Righteous behavior, even when done for the wrong reason, is better than unrighteous behavior. But a sinner who recognizes his need of God's mercy is more pleasing to God than a prideful religious person.

In spending time with non-Christians, we walk in the footsteps of Christ. We make His pattern our pattern and His practice our practice. To be Christlike, we must spend time with non-Christians.

What if Christians had avoided us when we were non-Christians?

Think about how you came to Christ. Most likely, a Christian spent time with you, and ultimately shared the gospel with you. Would you have been interested in what that person said if you didn't know that he or she cared? Concern led to conversation, and conversation led to Christ. Suppose that person had agreed with, "Don't spend time with non-Christians." That would have prevented the relationship that God used to bring you to Him.

In Luke 6:31, Jesus Christ said, "And just as you want men to do to you, you also do to them likewise." A proper application would be, "If you're glad people spent time with you as a non-Christian, do also to others." As friendships with Christians brought us to Christ, our friendships with the lost can bring them to the Savior.

How deep is one's spiritual life if it goes downhill around non-Christians?

The term Paul used most to depict the spiritual life is *walk*. In Romans 6:4, for example, Paul writes, "Therefore we were buried with Him through baptism into death, that just as Christ was raised from the dead by the glory of the Father, even so we also should *walk* in newness of life." In Galatians 5:16 Paul says, "*Walk* in the Spirit, and you shall not fulfill the lust of the flesh" (emphases added). The depth of our spiritual lives shouldn't be determined by the circumstances in which we walk. But that walk is to be so centered in Him that the Christ with whom we walk empowers our spiritual lives. As we walk with Christ, we set a pattern for others to follow. We do not follow them. That's why Paul could say in 1 Corinthians 11:1, "Imitate me, just as I also imitate Christ."

Why does walking with Christ enhance my spiritual growth regardless of the situation I'm in? Christ never changes, even when circumstances do. With Christ, I can live on the highest level even in the lowest of circumstances. If our spiritual lives slide when we're around non-Christians, then we are other-directed, not Christ-directed.

What is really at issue?

In Scripture, the word fellowship is used of a relationship between believers. The apostle John testified, "That which we have seen and heard we declare to you, that you also may have fellowship with us; and truly our fellowship is with the Father and with His Son Jesus Christ" (1 John 1:3). That close fellowship is so important that we are cautioned not to forsake it. The writer of Hebrews exhorts, "And let us consider one another in order to stir up love and good works, not forsaking the assembling of ourselves together, as is the manner of some, but exhorting one another, and so much the more as you see the Day approaching" (Heb. 10:24–25).

Christ's own example, though, shows that contact is encouraged in our relationships with lost people. Why did Christ eat at the home of Zacchaeus? He explained, "For the Son of Man has come to seek and to save that which was lost" (Luke 19:10). Through that contact, a relationship is established in which the gospel is shared and people come to the Savior.

The biblical position would be this: Have *communion* with believers; have *contact* with unbelievers. We have close fellowship with believers as we encourage one another. We pray together, share the Lord's supper together, worship, and study Scripture together. While keeping close communion with the saved, we retain contact with those who are not saved. Will that contact also be close? At times. But we can't be as close with unbelievers as we are with believers who have the same new nature and know the same Savior. That's why 2 Corinthians 6:14 warns, "Do not be unequally yoked together with unbelievers. For what fellowship has righteousness with lawlessness? And what communion has light with darkness?" Since believers and non-believers do not share a Savior in common, they cannot have the close communion that exists between believers.

Through communion with Christians and contact with non-Christians, we honor our responsibilities within the body of Christ. We also keep the proper relationship with those who are not yet part of His family. In our relationships with Christians and non-Christians, we obey Christ's words and example.

Conclusion

The Bible doesn't forbid keeping company with sinners. First Corinthians 5:9 encourages us to stay away from immoral *believers*, not immoral unbelievers. James 4:4, in discussing friendship with the world as being at enmity with God, does not forbid contact with non-Christians, but James cautions us to influence the world, not to let the world influence us. We must be a friend of sinners if we are to lead them to Christ.

> **The Bible doesn't forbid keeping company with sinners. It encourages it. Personal evangelism necessitates personal contact.**

Misconception 4

"If you want to be saved, just invite Jesus into your heart."

((•))

A woman seeking a divorce went before the judge. He asked, "On what grounds do you want a divorce?" She replied, "My husband and I own an acre and a half of ground. I'd like the divorce to cover the whole thing." The judge said, "No, you don't understand. I mean, do you have a grudge?" She said, "Yes, we have a two-car one. He keeps his car on the left, and I keep mine on the right." The judge asked, "No, what I mean is, does he ever beat you up?" The woman replied, "No, I'm up at least an hour before him every morning. Not once has he ever beat me up." The judge in desperation exclaimed, "I don't understand. What is the reason you want a divorce?" She said, "I don't understand it either. He says that I can't communicate."

Word choice is important to communication. Well-intentioned believers want to communicate the need to come to Christ and be saved. To do that, especially with children, they beg non-Christians to "invite Jesus into your heart."

There's a problem, though. That phrase isn't found in the Bible. Only one verse could be considered to support such wording. Let's examine it in context.

Where does such a phrase originate?

Revelation 3:20, reads "Behold, I stand at the door and knock. If anyone hears My voice and opens the door, I will come in to him and dine with him, and he with Me." With that phrase in mind—"stand at the door and knock"—many picture the heart as having a door. As Jesus knocks on that door, He begs us to let Him in. So the lost are exhorted to "invite Jesus into your heart." The problem is, that verse is addressed to Christians, not non-Christians.

Consider the context. The preceding verse reads, "As many as I love, I rebuke and chasten." *Chasten* means to train a child and is used throughout the New Testament of believers, not unbelievers. For example, the same word for *chasten* is used in Hebrews 12:5–6: "And you have forgotten the exhortation which speaks to you as to sons: 'My son, do not despise the chastening of the LORD, nor be discouraged when you are rebuked by Him; for whom the LORD loves He chastens, and scourges every son whom He receives." Revelation 3:20 is also addressed to Christians and concerns their fellowship with the Lord; it's not to non-Christians concerning their salvation.

To be specific, this passage addresses the church of Laodicea, one of the seven churches of Asia mentioned in Revelation 2 and 3. The city was founded by Antiochus II and named after his wife, Laodice. With a profitable business arising from the production of wool cloth, Laodicea became wealthy. So wealthy that, when destroyed by an earthquake in A.D. 60, it was able to rebuild without outside help. That economic sufficiency lulled the church into a spiritual sleep.

Jesus Christ describes this distasteful condition as "lukewarm," neither cold nor hot toward spiritual matters. To such a church, as well as to all the churches mentioned in Revelation, Christ gives the invitation of Revelation 3:20. He represents Himself to the churches and the people within as standing outside the door awaiting an invitation to enter. He desires them to repent of their condition and make Him the center of their worship and love.

Two other things are worth noting. In Revelation 3:20, the Greek translation of *in to* means "toward." In figurative language, Jesus is saying to Christians that He will enter the church and come toward the believer for fellowship. Secondly, the word *dine* refers to the main meal of the day, to which you invited an honored guest. This would not be peanut butter and jelly sandwiches eaten hurriedly at the kitchen counter. More likely, it would be roast beef with tender carrots, potatoes, and gravy. It was the meal given over to hospitality and conversation. Had you said to my wife and me, "Come dine with us" and used this word, we would have known two things: you meant the evening meal, and you wanted to fellowship across the table. Jesus' offer, then, was one of intimate fellowship.

Revelation 3:20 is addressed to Christians, inviting them to "open the door" and allow Christ to enter into close fellowship. It is addressed to Christians and concerns their fellowship with Christ, not to non-Christians concerning their salvation.

What term or phrase does the Bible use to mean "salvation"?

In evangelizing the lost, speak the language the Bible speaks. The book of John explains how to receive the gift of eternal life. John, in fact, identifies the purpose of his book: "But these are written that you may believe that Jesus is the Christ, the Son of God, and that believing you may have life in His name" (20:31).

How does one receive that eternal life? The word that John uses ninety-eight times is *believe.* Prior to raising Martha's brother, Lazarus, from the grave, Christ explained to her, "I am the resurrection and the life. He who believes in Me, though he may die, he shall live. And whoever lives and believes in Me shall never die" (John 11:25–26). *Believe* means, "Understanding that Jesus Christ died for me and rose again, I receive eternal life by trusting Him alone as my only way to heaven."

A woman who attended a liberal church once asked her pastor, "If I watch a John Wayne movie, is God more likely to let me into heaven?" She sincerely thought that John Wayne was a good friend of Jesus Christ and watching one of his movies would increase her chance of getting into heaven. We might laugh at her logic, but we're just as mistaken to think that church attendance, baptism, keeping the commandments, taking the sacraments, or any amount of good living can get us into heaven. God asks us to trust a *person*—Jesus Christ—as our only means of salvation.

Does the Bible use other terms to convey the idea of appropriation? Consider the following:

- Nicodemus was told to look and live (John 3:14–15).
- The Samaritan woman was told to ask (John 4:10).
- The Jews were told to come to Christ (John 5:40).
- The multitudes were told to believe in Christ (John 6:47).
- They were also told to eat His flesh and drink His blood (John 6:53–54). Note: This is in the context of Christ being the "Bread of Life" (cf. John 6:35).
- The Pharisees were told to keep His Word (John 8:51).
- Others were told to look at Christ as a door and enter in (John 10:9).

Each contains the idea of appropriation. The thought conveyed is, "Recognizing that Christ alone is my only way to eternal life, I take Him at His Word and trust Him to save me."

The gospel of John never exhorts one to "invite Jesus into your heart." The phrase is not used in Scripture in evangelizing the lost.

What's the danger in using "invite Jesus into your heart"?

When someone uses the phrase "invite Jesus into your heart," the thought often conveyed is "Say a prayer that 'invites Jesus into your heart' and you're saved." A person places trust in a prayer that was said instead of the Savior who died on a cross.

While I was speaking in one community, a couple invited me to dinner. As she set the table and took the bread out of the oven, the woman said, "I had a very exciting day. Two children called and asked, 'What do you have to do to get to heaven?' I told them, 'Just bow your heads right now and let's invite Jesus into your heart.'" As I questioned her, I learned that she never even mentioned Christ's death and resurrection. The thought conveyed was that a person received eternal life by saying a prayer.

During an outreach in Michigan, I said, "I'd like to speak to anyone who isn't certain that if you were to die you'd go to heaven." A man who had preached passionately in missions all over the city approached me. I asked, "Why did you respond?" He said, "I want to dedicate my life to Christ." But he seemed hesitant. So I said, "Before we talk about that, let me ask you something. Do you know beyond any doubt that if you were to die right now you'd go to heaven?" The tall, slender young man answered, "Yeah, uh-huh." I sensed uncertainty. At this point, had I backed off, he probably would have too. But I continued, "If I asked you, 'How did *you* become a Christian?' what would you say?" He explained that when he was young he bowed his head and invited Jesus into his heart. I asked, "Based on my message tonight, if I asked you, 'What must I do to get to heaven?' what would you tell me?" He answered, "I'd tell you that you have to understand that you're a sinner, that Jesus Christ died for you and arose, and that trust in Christ alone is your only way to heaven." I said, "Why is it that you just had to invite Him into your heart, but *I* have to *trust* Him?" He broke down and said, "Quite honestly, I've never understood this before. I thought that if you said a prayer inviting Jesus into your heart that God would let you into heaven because you said it. I had no idea that you had to trust in Jesus Christ alone as your only way to heaven."

The phrase "invite Jesus into your heart" often conveys the idea that one is saved by saying a prayer instead of trusting Christ. Such a thought is not biblical. It's also illogical. A woman told me how God taught her the danger of such a phrase. She invited a child to "ask Jesus into your heart." He said, "It wouldn't do any good." "Why?" she asked. He answered, "Mommy says there's a hole in my heart. If I invite Him in, He'll just fall out."

Has no one ever been saved when the phrase "invite Jesus into your heart" has been used? It's beyond doubt that many have said such a prayer, understanding they were trusting Christ alone to save them. They understood they were saved by trusting Christ, not by saying a prayer. Many, though, have "invited Christ into their hearts," not understanding that the issue is trusting Christ alone to save them.

What invitation should we offer non-Christians?

God desires that we proclaim the gospel clearly. He longs for all to understand His Son's announcement, "It is finished" (John 19:30). We should ask people to do what the New Testament asks them to do— "believe." We can then explain that *believe* means we come to God as sinners, recognize that Christ died for us and arose, and trust in Christ alone to save us. The best word to convey what the Bible means by *believe* is the word *trust.* Trusting Christ is not merely accepting intellectually that a person named Jesus Christ died on a cross and rose again. It is acknowledging that He alone is my only way to heaven. Trusting Christ is the means through which we appropriate His gift of eternal life.

Explain to non-Christians that all of us are sinners. The punishment for that sin is death and eternal separation from God. Jesus Christ satisfied the anger of God against our sin by taking the punishment we deserve and rising from the grave the third day. We should then invite the lost to trust in Christ alone. Upon trusting Christ, they are as certain of heaven as though they are already there.

Conclusion

Word choice is important in communicating clearly. The plan of salvation is too crucial to communicate any other way. The phrase "invite Jesus into your heart" is not used in Scripture in inviting the lost to be saved. Because it is not used in Scripture and because it encourages people to think that one is saved by saying a prayer, it should not be used in evangelism. The one verse that infers the thought of "invite Jesus into your heart" speaks to Christians about fellowship.

We should do what the Bible encourages us to do. We should invite the lost to believe, to trust in Christ alone for salvation.

> The phrase "invite Jesus into your heart" is not used in Scripture. The Bible asks us to believe—to appropriate Christ's finished work on the cross by trusting Him alone to save us.

Misconception 5

"When you miss an opportunity to share Christ with someone, it's your fault if that person goes to hell."

$((\bullet))$

I knew she could do it. Others told me so. Women like her were needed to speak to non-Christian women. Her frequent short-term mission trips had given her opportunities.

But something troubled her. Through a veil of tears, she told me what it was. The more she talked, the more I fought anger, frustration, and pity. A misconception had caused her unnecessary suffering. Using Scripture, I set her free. Then I asked her to write about the misconception so I could use it to help others. Here's what she said:

"Coming from the background I did, I'm guilt-oriented when it comes to evangelism. I feel so badly about it no matter what! If I talk to someone about Christ, I worry that I didn't do it 'good enough.' If I resist an opportunity to share Christ, I feel condemned, like a lousy Christian. When I was a new Christian in college, a preacher said, 'If you don't share Christ with someone, their blood is on your hands.' To some people, that may be motivating, but to me it was just more guilt and condemnation."

That thought—"When you miss an opportunity to share Christ with someone, it's your fault if that person goes to hell"—is often communicated. The actual terminology used is, "Their blood is on your hands." Her observation was accurate—to some, that phrase might be motivating, but it usually instills guilt. That guilt is accompanied by pressure, fear, and shame. What could be worse than thinking that a person you failed to witness to is now in hell, that it's your fault, that their blood is on your hands?

I became numb and nauseated reading a letter from my family in Pennsylvania. My friend Ray had been murdered. Ray had stopped one night to collect rent in the apartment complex that he owned. The two men who answered the knock asked him to step inside. Overtaking him, they stabbed him more than a dozen times, spilling blood on the carpet and splattering it on the wallpaper. After stuffing his body in a black, plastic garbage bag, they dumped it along a country road. Their prison sentence? Seventeen years, with good behavior. Their actual sentence? If their conscience bothers them at all, it's living the rest of their lives knowing a woman was a widow, a family was fatherless, friends were stunned. They would never be able to erase the night, the knife, the pleading screams of a dying man.

If the above misconception is true, though, there's a greater horror than knowing you caused someone's death. It's the horror of knowing you were responsible for someone's eternal torment in hell.

Imagine your friend in hell, isolated, burning, thirsting in a dark, empty, sulfuric space. He longs for a touch, cries out for relief, craves one sip. He yearns to die but cannot. He searches for a face, a sound, anything. He recalls every missed opportunity, every relationship, every rejection. A scream pierces the air and he discovers it is his own. He is in hell. And if this misconception is correct, it's your fault because you didn't tell him about Christ.

What Scripture is used to support this misconception?

Ezekiel 3:18–19 is often taken out of context: "When I say to the wicked, 'You shall surely die,' and you give him no warning, nor speak to warn the wicked from his wicked way, to save his life, that same wicked man shall die in his iniquity; but his blood I will require at your hand. Yet, if you warn the wicked, and he does not turn from his wickedness, nor from his wicked way, he shall die in his iniquity; but you have delivered your soul."

God appointed Ezekiel a watchman. Two verses earlier we read, "Now it came to pass at the end of seven days that the word of the Lord came to me, saying, 'Son of man, I have made you a watchman for the house of Israel; therefore hear a word from My mouth, and give them warning from Me" (vv. 16–17). A watchman alerted the city of coming danger. He stood on the city wall, hilltop, or watchtower, guarding against threat. If he failed, the city could be lost. Ezekiel's job was to warn of impending danger. The nation was doomed. Only through heeding their watchman could they survive. Chapters 4–24 of Ezekiel contain his cry of alarm, which gave those outside the walls an opportunity to seek protection. It also gave the people time to secure the gates and man the defenses.

The death spoken of in Ezekiel 3:18–19 is physical, not spiritual. The context is the Babylonian destruction of Jerusalem that Ezekiel predicted. The wicked person refusing to heed God's warning could expect physical death.

Examining the verses in context, Ezekiel was to warn the righteous, not just the wicked. Verses 20–21 tell us,

> Again, when a righteous man turns from his righteousness and commits iniquity, and I lay a stumbling block before him, he shall die; because you did not give him warning, he shall die in his sin, and his righteousness which he has done shall not be remembered; but his blood I will require at your hand. Nevertheless if you warn the righteous man that the righteous should not sin, and he does not sin, he shall surely live because he took warning; also you will have delivered your soul.

As Nebuchadnezzar's armies approached, the righteous person departing from the path of righteousness was also in danger. That didn't mean the person lost eternal salvation.

Again, the death spoken of here is physical death. God's judgment was about to fall on Jerusalem. Those breaking His commandments could expect the physical consequences of sin.

Ezekiel's warnings were not general principles, but specific revelations. He was made mute by God until God gave him the specific message, and he could only speak when God told him to. When his speechlessness was removed, he pronounced the prophecies. Ezekiel 3:26–27 tells us,

> I will make your tongue cling to the roof of your mouth, so that you shall be mute and not be one to rebuke them, for they are a rebellious house. But when I speak with you, I will open your mouth, and you shall say to them, "Thus says the Lord God." He who hears, let him hear; and he who refuses, let him refuse; for they are a rebellious house.

This temporary muteness remained with Ezekiel until the fall of Jerusalem. At that time the prophecies he had delivered were confirmed. We are told in Ezekiel 33:21–22,

> And it came to pass in the twelfth year of our captivity, in the tenth month, on the fifth day of the month, that one who had escaped from Jerusalem came to me and said, "The city has been captured!" Now the hand of the LORD had been upon me the evening before the man came who had escaped. And He had opened my mouth; so when he came to me in the morning, my mouth was opened, and I was no longer mute.

What if Ezekiel refused to speak God's message to the people who came to his house? He would be guilty of murder. This is the meaning of "his blood I will require at your hand"; God would hold Ezekiel accountable. He would be as responsible for their deaths as if he had killed them himself. Once more, the blood had nothing to do with spiritual death, but physical death. What if Ezekiel fulfilled his responsibility in warning them, even if they neglected his warning? He would save himself. The word *saved* means delivered and does not refer to eternal salvation. By giving a warning, Ezekiel delivered himself from responsibility for the coming judgment. Those who ignored his warning could only blame themselves.

What's the problem when we apply "blood on your hands" to evangelism?

As you can see, Ezekiel 3:18–19 does not apply to evangelism. The New Testament believer is not a "watchman" over the world. Today's watchmen are the Holy Spirit and the Word of God.

In John 16, Christ declared of the Holy Spirit,

> It is to your advantage that I go away; for if I do not go away, the Helper will not come to you; but if I depart, I will send Him to you. And when He has come, He will convict the world of sin, and of righteousness, and of judgment: of sin, because they do not believe in Me; of righteousness, because I go to My Father and you see Me no more; of judgment, because the ruler of this world is judged. (John 16:7–11)

Concerning the Scriptures, 2 Timothy 3:16–17 tells us, "All Scripture is given by inspiration of God, and is profitable for doctrine, for reproof, for correction, for instruction in righteousness, that the man of God may be complete, thoroughly equipped for every good work."

The death we speak of to the lost is not merely physical death; it is spiritual death, eternal separation from God. Hebrews 9:27 warns of the eternal death that is beyond physical death for the non-Christian: "And as it is appointed for men to die once, but after this the judgment." Any warnings about this judgment are derived from the Word, not specific revelations.

Our failure to evangelize may mean loss of reward when we see the Savior, but it won't mean God will charge us with murder.

Why is it not "our fault" if someone goes to hell?

God is in complete control, not partial control. He is sovereign, and that sovereignty extends to salvation. Paul testified, "For whom He foreknew, He also predestined to be conformed to the image of His Son, that He might be the firstborn among many brethren. Moreover whom He predestined, these He also called; whom He called, these He also justified; and whom He justified, these He also glorified" (Rom. 8:29–30).

In Misconception 17—"Since I, God, am sovereign and will save whomever I choose, I don't need your help"—we'll examine God's sovereignty more carefully. The point here is that the blood of non-Christians is not on our hands because God is in control. It is He, not us, who foreknows, predestines, calls, justifies, and glorifies.

Romans 3:11 tells us, "There is none who seeks after God." Non-Christians cannot come to God unless He brings them. If they come to Christ, He has to draw them. When Jesus confronted the ignorance of His own people, who rejected Him, He recognized their inability to remove that blindness. He testified, "No one can come to Me unless the Father who sent Me draws him; and I will raise him up at the last day" (John 6:44).

God is sovereign over everything including salvation. We should strive not to fail in our responsibility to evangelize, but if we do fail, it's not our fault if nonbelievers go to hell. Although He desires to use us, each person's destiny is in God's hands.

Conclusion

Using Ezekiel 3:18–19 in evangelism is not a proper handling of Scripture. God was speaking to Ezekiel about his responsibility as a watchman to the nation of Israel; He was not speaking about your responsibility as a witness. Yes, some passages may be understood in context and then *applied* to evangelism, but the Ezekiel passage is not one of them. God's sovereignty over the salvation of each individual leaves the results in His hands, not ours.

> **There are many motivations to evangelize. The Ezekiel passage referring to "blood on our hands" is not one of them. God does not fault us with anyone's eternal destiny.**

"If you're going to evangelize, you must know how to defend what you believe."

((•))

A neighbor says, "I don't believe the Bible."

A coworker says, "I don't think Christ was who He said He was."

Your sister says, "Christians are hypocrites."

Intimidating objections, aren't they? Can we evangelize if we can't answer those objections?

A brochure for an evangelism conference caught my attention, especially the first topic—"How to answer objections."

I said to myself, "Wait a minute. This is a conference on evangelism. They want to excite people about sharing the gospel, yet they begin with, 'How to answer objections.' People will think they have to answer every objection a non-Christian raises. This brochure scares believers before they get started." I thought about how often I fly. Many people are scared to step on a plane. How many would ever get on a plane if they were reminded of everything that could go wrong?

I think I know why answering objections was the first topic. The idea often conveyed is, "If you're going to evangelize you must be able to defend what you believe." I've even heard people say, "If you can't, you'd better not evangelize."

That thought is a misconception, and one Bible verse in particular is used to support that misconception.

Where does this thought originate?

First Peter 3:15 reads, "But sanctify the Lord God in your hearts, and always be ready to give a defense to everyone who asks you a reason for the hope that is in you, with meekness and fear." The phrase "always be ready to give a defense to everyone who asks you" leads some to think that, in order to evangelize, they must be able to defend what they believe in.

What, though, is the context of Peter's statement? Peter was writing about honoring God regardless of what life does to you. A prime opportunity is when suffering for doing right.

Peter began, "And who is he who will harm you if you become followers of what is good?" (v. 13). People usually don't harm those who do good. They harm those who do evil. Peter adds, though, "But even if you should suffer for righteousness' sake, you are blessed. And do not be afraid of their threats, nor be troubled." If you suffer for doing right, don't be intimidated or upset.

That's easier said than done. When suffering for what is right, how do you *not* be intimidated? Peter's answer was, "But sanctify the Lord God in your hearts." *Sanctify* means "set apart," so set apart the Lord God in your hearts. A proper fear of God ought to drive out your fear of man.

Early church Christians were hearing rumors about persecution in parts of the Roman empire. Believers were thrown to lions and burned at the stake. Those were the gentler, quicker deaths. Nero, head of the Roman empire, dipped Christians into sticky, black pitch, set them on fire, and used them as torches to light his gardens. He sewed them in the skins of wild animals and set his hunting dogs upon them to tear them to death. Others were tortured, molten lead poured onto them. Red-hot brass plates were affixed to the most tender parts of their bodies. Their eyes were ripped out. Their hands and feet were burned while cold water was poured over them to lengthen the agony. Their suffering was horrific, yet Peter said, "Don't be afraid of their threats. Don't be troubled."

Peter was quoting Isaiah 8:12–13, which reads, "Do not say, 'A conspiracy,' concerning all that this people call a conspiracy, nor be afraid of their threats, nor be troubled. The LORD of hosts, Him you shall hallow; let Him be your fear, and let Him be your dread." The Israelites were unable to trust God in the shadow of invasion, so God urged the prophets not to share their own fears. Instead they were to trust God. Peter, too, urged his readers to so make the Lord the focus of their hearts that all other fears were set aside.

What would be the outcome? Peter continued, "And always be ready to give a defense to everyone who asks you a reason for the hope that is in you, with meekness and fear." When you suffer for doing right and refuse to be intimidated, people want to know why. It's then that you can give every man who asks you a reason for the hope that is in you. The phrase "give a defense" is the translation of a Greek word used as a legal term in a court of law. It refers to the intelligent reply given by an attorney when speaking on behalf of his client. That reply ought to be accompanied by meekness and fear, meaning humility toward men and reverence toward God.

The problem with how that verse has been used to discourage evangelizing is obvious. Nowhere in 1 Peter 3:15 is there a *hint* that we must be able to defend what we believe in order to evangelize. That's not the context of the paragraph. Nor should that verse be used to support the need for apologetics, as helpful as apologetics is. Instead, it is an uplifting thought that helps us respond properly when suffering for doing right. With intelligence and humility, give those who oppose you a reason for the hope that is in you. First Peter 3:15 infers that suffering for doing what is right offers opportunity to speak on behalf of the Savior. In no way, though, does it declare we must defend what we believe in order to evangelize.

Examine Paul's comments about his ministry in Corinth and Athens.

Paul knew how to defend what he believed. He grew up in Tarsus, a city noted for its intellectuals, and his knowledge of Roman law and custom was second to none. He'd mastered the Greek language, and he'd studied under Gamaliel, one of the most distinguished teachers of his day. On a panel, Paul could have debated the best; confronted with an atheist, he could have laid out the proof for the existence of God.

That's why his remarks in 1 Corinthians 2:1–2 are striking. He explained, "And I, brethren, when I came to you, did not come with excellence of speech or of wisdom declaring to you the testimony of God. For I determined not to know anything among you except Jesus Christ and Him crucified." His words "for I determined" indicate a before-thought not an afterthought. His decision was made one mile from the city, not one mile inside the city. Corinth was filled with intellectuals and philosophers who loved to discuss and debate. But when Paul entered the city, the first thing he told the Corinthians was the good news of the gospel. He preached "Christ and Him crucified." He didn't enter the city *defending* what he believed. He entered *declaring* what he believed.

His approach didn't change before a similar audience in Athens. One verse summarizes his ministry strategy when confronted with the philosophers: "Then certain Epicurean and Stoic philosophers encountered him. And some said, 'What does this babbler want to say?' Others said, 'He seems to be a proclaimer of foreign gods,' because he preached to them Jesus and the resurrection" (Acts 17:18).

In both Corinth and Athens, Paul proclaimed Christ. He believed that God wanted him to declare Christ rather than defend Him.

New believers who cannot yet defend what they believe lead the largest number of unbelievers to Christ.

New believers lead more people to Christ than any other group. Thrilled to have found the answer, they are convinced the whole world needs to know Him. Most of their acquaintances are unbelievers. Boldly and enthusiastically, new believers tell their many lost friends about Christ.

Being new Christians, they don't have a lot of Bible knowledge. They tell their lost friends the only message they know: "Christ died for your sins and arose. Through personal trust in Him you can receive His gift of eternal life." How much deeper into the message can they go? Can they explain why the Scriptures are without error? Can they defend the deity of Christ and lay out the historical proof behind the Resurrection? Can they explain the three persons of the Trinity? Hardly ever! If defending what we believe is essential to evangelism, then new believers couldn't lead their acquaintances to Christ.

Recently, I read of a man whose conversion was so dramatic that people noticed a change in his life. Over the next fourteen months, he led more than one hundred people to the Savior. All he knew was the simple message of the gospel. Even as I was writing this chapter, a pastor told me of a new convert leading many to Christ. He just kept taking lost people to the only verse he knew—John 3:16!

All non-Christians don't have the same struggles.

People approach Christianity with different questions. Some struggle with the idea that Jesus Christ is the Son of God. Some question whether the Bible is what it claims to be—the Word of God. Others feel that what Christ has to offer is only for the "down and out." Why should any respectable person need a Savior? How can you call Him a God of love when children die young and adults suffer agonizing deaths?

If we say, "You must be able to defend what you believe before you can evangelize," even a mature believer wouldn't know where to start. No one can be certain which objection a non-Christian will raise.

Chuck, a good friend of mine, was talking with a client and asked, "Are you interested in spiritual things?" The client spouted his anger toward God. As a child, he begged God to make his father stop beating his mother and siblings. The bruises were temporary—his anger and insecurity lasted decades. According to this man, "God never answered my prayers." Chuck asked, "Do you think God was responsible for those beatings?" The man responded, "Well . . . no. My dad was." Chuck then asked, "So why are you blaming God?" He couldn't answer. Chuck then said, "Would you like to know beyond any doubt that if you were to die you'd go straight to heaven?" The man confessed that he would. So Chuck said, "Suppose you were to stand before God and He were to ask, 'Why should I let you into heaven?' what would you tell Him?" The man responded, "I'd tell Him I've lived a good life." Chuck took the Bible and, using our Bad News/Good News approach (see Appendix), explained the gospel. The man trusted Christ, and all of this happened within an hour. The new convert later told Chuck about the dramatic changes in his life. When he began talking about salvation, Chuck didn't know which objection that man would raise or where the interaction would lead. But he didn't allow himself to be dragged into a defensive posture. Instead, he seized the opportunity to declare the good news of Christ.

Shouldn't we defend what we believe?

Is it sometimes helpful to defend what you believe? The answer is *yes*. Many non-Christians say, "But I don't believe the Bible," when confronted with the gospel. A new Christian might think, "What more can I say? If this person doesn't believe the Bible, the discussion is closed." A person evangelizing can, though, use a powerful response to that objection. Although the Bible is indeed the Word of God, the support for Christianity reaches beyond the Bible. It stands or falls on the resurrection of Christ. When all the evidence behind the resurrection is collected, it becomes the most attested to fact of history. It's wise to say, "Oh, but the proof for Christianity goes beyond the Bible. It rests on the empty tomb of Christ. Even atheists haven't been able to deny that supernatural event. Give the empty tomb an honest and objective evaluation. Before you dismiss Christ, you must be able to disprove the Resurrection—something no one has ever done." That puts the focus where it needs to be. It forces the hearer to consider, "Am I willing to examine the evidence for Christianity?"

Knowing how to respond to objections is helpful, but it's inaccurate to say that one must be able to do so in order to evangelize. Supporting such a thought from the Bible is a mishandling of the Scriptures.

Conclusion

Being able to defend what we believe is helpful in evangelism. It's a skill to develop. But the Bible doesn't teach that to evangelize you must know how to defend what you believe. New believers lead more people to Christ than anyone else because they know the simple truth—Christ died for our sins and arose. God uses this zealous proclamation to bring multitudes to Christ.

> **Being able to defend what you believe is helpful in evangelism. But the Bible doesn't teach that believers must be able to defend what they believe before they can evangelize.**

Misconception 7

"If evangelism scares you, you don't have the gift of evangelism."

$((\bullet))$

You walk into Krispy Kreme for a dozen sugar-glazed donuts. The owners are cordial, and ask after your wife and kids. The music coming through the radio speakers gives you an opportunity to turn the conversation to spiritual things. Friends have told you that you probably have the gift of evangelism, but as you stand there, you're afraid to mention Christ. Your hands are clammy. Your throat is dry. Your heart races. Does that mean you don't have the gift of evangelism?

Many believe that if they feel fear when attempting to evangelize, then they don't have the gift. They've said, "I think I may have the gift of evangelism. But sometimes I'm scared to death, so apparently I don't."

Is that true? If someone experiences fear in evangelism, does it mean that person doesn't have the gift of evangelism? Does the presence of fear indicate the absence of gift?

What is the gift of evangelism?

One might ask, "What is the gift of evangelism? Doesn't every Christian have a responsibility to evangelize?" In speaking of spiritually gifted people, Ephesians 4:11 reads, "And He Himself gave some to be apostles, some prophets, and some evangelists, and some pastors and teachers. . . ." What does the evangelist gift involve?

Our English word *evangel* comes from the Greek word *euangelion* meaning "good news." Therefore, the term *evangelist* means "one who announces the good news of Christ's death and resurrection." If all we had was the Greek word we'd know that evangelism is the ability to preach the gospel.

But that's not all we have. Examining the context of Ephesians 4:11 we must ask, "Why does God give these gifted people to the body of Christ?" We're told one verse later: "For the equipping of the saints for the work of ministry, for the edifying of the body of Christ." The gift of evangelism, then, not only involves outreach to the lost but also an edification ministry to believers. The evangelist's gift centers in the gospel, so it's safe to assume that, in assisting the believers, evangelists are to teach them how to evangelize effectively. Hence, the gift of the evangelist has two prongs—reaching the non-Christian and equipping the believer.

Not everyone has such a gift. That doesn't change the fact that all believers have a *responsibility* to evangelize. The first thing Christ taught His disciples was, "Follow Me, and I will make you fishers of men" (Matt. 4:19). Although all who would be His disciples have a responsibility to evangelize, not all have the gift of evangelism.

An analogy to the gift of evangelism is the gift of giving. All believers have a responsibility to give. Second Corinthians 9:7 reminds us, "So let each one give as he purposes in his heart, not grudgingly or of necessity; for God loves a cheerful giver." Yet some have a special God-given ability to give—they give of their resources to benefit others, and they find great joy in doing so. Likewise, all Christians have a responsibility to evangelize. Some have a special God-given ability in sharing Christ and find great fulfillment as they do.

Back to the question, "Does the presence of fear in evangelism indicate an absence of the gift of evangelism?"

Understanding the gift of evangelism, we can now examine the question, "Does the presence of fear indicate the absence of the gift?"

As Scripture addresses the gift, the subject of fear is not mentioned. It is, again, a two-pronged gift, a reaching ministry to the non-Christian and an equipping ministry to the believer. Looking at both purposes of the gift, fear is not addressed.

The only evangelist mentioned in Scripture is Philip. In Acts 8, as he presented Christ to the Ethiopian eunuch (vv. 26–39), he was acting under specific instructions: The Spirit of God directed him, "Go near and overtake this chariot" (v. 29). The text tells us, "So Philip ran to him, and heard him reading the prophet Isaiah, and said, 'Do you understand what you are reading?'" The Ethiopian was a receptive audience, and he answered, "How can I, unless someone guides me?" (vv. 30–31). In that situation, there was no reason for fear. We can't determine if Philip would have been afraid had his audience been more hostile.

Evangelists are not supernatural people. They are *normal* people with a *supernatural* gift. What do normal people fear as they evangelize? Paul, who evangelized even though his gift was apparently pastor-teacher, offers insight. Describing his ministry in Corinth, he said, "And I, brethren, when I came to you, did not come with excellence of speech or of wisdom declaring to you the testimony of God. For I determined not to know anything among you except Jesus Christ and Him crucified. I was with you in weakness, in fear, and in much trembling" (1 Cor. 2:1–3).

Weakness could refer to everything from his thorn in the flesh (whatever troubled him physically, cf. 2 Cor. 12:7) to his absence of physical strength due to his unimpressive build. In physique, Paul wouldn't have struck you as a guy who works out at the gym. He may not have been as frail as some portray him, but neither would he have been linebacker material for the NFL.

Fear could refer to everything from the wickedness of the city, which made him unpopular, to the hostility of the Jews, which made him unwanted. At times Paul knew that he had friends; at times he likely searched for friends. What better word than "fears" would describe his feelings?

Trembling probably refers to his body quivering with nervousness.

If you watched Paul declare the gospel, you may have walked away saying, "He seemed a bit nervous."

Now consider Ephesians 6:19. What two prayer requests did Paul give his brothers and sisters in the body of Christ? He asked, ". . . that utterance may be given to me, that I may open my mouth boldly to make known the mystery of the gospel." The two requests are for utterance and boldness. "That utterance may be given to me" has the idea of "when I open my mouth something comes out." Paul was evidently concerned he'd be unable to get the words out. "That I may open my mouth boldly" could be translated, "That what comes out might come out boldly." Paul's desire, then, was not merely to be a proclaimer of the gospel but a *bold* proclaimer.

Why would someone who was *not* experiencing fear ask for prayer in those two areas? Without the presence of fear those prayer requests are meaningless. So we can safely conclude that Paul faced fear in evangelism. As he evangelized, though, he prayed and others prayed for him. As a result, boldness overtook fear instead of fear overtaking boldness.

As this close look at Scripture shows, neither a godly character nor the spiritual gift of evangelism can prevent us from being afraid.

Now examine gifted evangelists.

Our conclusions must always be from Scripture, not experience. At the same time, Scripture is verified by experience. The question to ask now is, "Have those respected as being gifted in evangelism ever admitted to being afraid?"

I've met gifted evangelists across the world. Many spoke of their reliance upon God to overcome their fears. I once spoke in Illinois and had lunch with the pastor and his wife and two couples from the church. As we dug into the roast beef and mashed potatoes, we also dug into conversation about evangelism. One of the women, by the pastor's observation and her own confession, had the gift of evangelism. She welcomed opportunities to evangelize as eagerly as would a woman gifted in hospitality welcome people into her home. She said,

"I believe I have the gift of evangelism and yet sometimes I'm afraid to share Christ. Can you offer anything that would help me overcome that fear?" I commended her for admitting her fear, even though she expressed no doubt that she had the gift of evangelism. I shared several things with her, stressing prayer, a method to share the gospel, and the importance of obedience.

Leighton Ford served for many years with the Billy Graham Association as a traveling evangelist. He once said, "I'm an evangelist, as I've been witnessing and sharing my faith since I was fourteen years old. I've preached to crowds of sixty thousand people, and yet I still get nervous when talking to an individual about Christ."

Billy Graham is respected as a gifted evangelist. I read his own testimony confessing fears he felt when sharing Christ one on one. I'm sure he'd agree that it often requires more courage to speak to one than to a thousand.

On a personal level, I've said many times, "If I couldn't share the gospel, why be alive?" To me it's exhilarating. Have there been times I've done so without fear? Yes, but those times have been the exception, not the norm. I usually experience fear due to the uncertainty of how the person will respond. Will that person be offended if I bring up the subject of spiritual things? Will this destroy a relationship? So I too feel nervousness, uncertainty, and fear. But every time I've asked God for boldness, I've experienced the courage I needed.

I flew from Dallas to El Paso a few weeks after September 11. The woman next to me was from Michigan, where she and her husband raised potatoes for Frito Lay. They were on their way to Mexico to install sophisticated equipment for producing potato chips. My farm background helped us relate to each other, and as I searched for a way to turn the conversation to spiritual things, I felt fear for two reasons. One was not knowing how she would respond. Pleasant as she was, I couldn't be sure that pleasantness would carry over into spiritual things. The other reason was her husband. He could overhear our conversation, and I wasn't certain he'd appreciate me talking to his wife about her need for Christ. I asked God for courage and began to sense His boldness. She mentioned how since September 11 "even the president can talk about prayer." That was my opportunity. I explained the gospel and gave her a tract, which I hoped God would use to bring her to Christ. There I was, gifted in evangelism and feeling fear. All I had to do was ask God for boldness.

What is the danger in thinking, "Those who have the gift of evangelism do not have fear"?

I believe many people are gifted in evangelism, but they don't realize it. People who have fear shouldn't use it as a basis to decide whether or not they have the gift. A person's spiritual gift is only developed through exercise and use, and basing a decision upon fear could keep that person from developing that gift. Instead, people should open themselves to the possibility of such a gift. Exposure to godly people and experience in Christian work will help such people determine if they have the gift. If they do, those people need to remember that evangelists sometimes experience fear as well.

Conclusion

"If evangelism scares you, you don't have the gift of evangelism" is not taught in Scripture. Those who have been gifted in evangelism also experience fear.

> **The presence of fear in evangelism doesn't mean the absence of the gift.**

Misconception 8

"If you don't shed tears for the lost, you won't be effective in evangelism."

((•))

Sincere. Frustrated. Confused. All three depicted the person behind the ink on the paper. Her letter expressed a frustration that many of us feel, although we might express it differently.

She wrote, "I've heard that unless we shed tears for the lost we cannot be effective in evangelism. How can we manufacture tears? I agree that we must have a genuine concern and compassion for the lost, for without the Savior, they are forever doomed to hell. But are tears necessary before the Lord will use us in evangelism?"

God doesn't convey that thought in the Bible. Like most misconceptions, that thought usually arises from people, not from a particular Scripture.

Who usually makes such a statement?

The statement "We must shed tears for the lost or we can never be effective in evangelism" is usually made by those who readily shed tears. Numerous people have said to me, "I cry easily." It's natural for them to cry on behalf of those who, without Christ, face an eternal hell.

Those who cry easily may have the gift of evangelism, which furthers their burden for the lost. Or they may have the gift of mercy, which makes them heartbroken for people in distress, including those who haven't met the Savior. Or they may have neither the gift of mercy nor the gift of evangelism, but a personality that lends itself to tears.

Years ago I met a very tenderhearted man—the kind who oozes compassion. When speaking of people's needs, he often became teary eyed. He once said, "Please forgive me. It bothers me that I cry so easily. It seems I can't help it." He had no need to apologize. While others might not cry as easily as he does, he's the tenderhearted man God made him to be. I comforted him, "Your tears are how you express your feelings." I don't know his spiritual gift, but I do know his temperament lends itself to tears.

Everyone I've met who made such a statement has been someone for whom tears come easily.

Biblically, are tears essential?

At the same time, it's wrong to make others feel guilty when they don't express their concern through tears. If a person isn't concerned about lost people going to hell, that *is* a problem. But if they don't grieve as someone else might or if they don't cry over a person's lost condition, that isn't a problem. The Bible doesn't say we have to shed tears to be used in evangelism. Who we are and what most excites or burdens us determines what makes us cry.

I have a friend with the gift of teaching. He doesn't just enjoy teaching. He's ecstatic about it. His eyes fill with tears when he talks about how a person's life was changed because of the things he taught. I'm an adjunct professor at two schools on a regular basis and teach at others as well. And, yes, it's rewarding to see truth impact attitudes about reaching the lost. I enjoy teaching and get excited about the results, but it doesn't stir my emotions the way I'm stirred when I plead with the lost to come to Christ. Evangelizing is more apt to make me teary-eyed than anything that happens while I'm teaching. The difference is one of gift.

A second example is my wife's gift of mercy—the ability to feel the hurts of others and help those in need. My wife hurts when others hurt. People with the gift of mercy often have that empathetic spirit, and they're so burdened over others that, if not careful, they take on the hurts of the whole world. My wife sheds tears easily for hurting people. A friend's marital problems make her weep. A young person struggling with drug addiction brings tears to her eyes. She'll cry over a baby who is born with a deformity. She's certainly concerned for lost people. Her tears, though, have more to do with their hurt than their lost condition. If she doesn't cry over their lost condition, even though I might, that doesn't mean she's unconcerned. Nor am I unconcerned for a hurting believer if my wife cries for them and I don't. Tears are not the issue, concern is.

The Bible doesn't say that tears are essential to be effective in evangelism. What generates tears is a personal matter—what excites or burdens us the most.

What does the Bible stress?

What we ought to feel for lost people is pity. Christ was filled with compassion, meaning that He pitied unbelievers. These eight passages show that pity:

1. "But when He saw the multitudes, He was moved with compassion for them, because they were weary and scattered, like sheep having no shepherd" (Matt. 9:36). The context is Christ's response to people in the cities and villages as He preached the gospel, taught in the synagogues, and healed the sick.
2. "And when Jesus went out He saw a great multitude; and He was moved with compassion for them, and healed their sick" (Matt. 14:14). The context is just prior to the feeding of the five thousand as multitudes followed Him to a deserted place outside the cities.
3. "Now Jesus called His disciples to Himself and said, 'I have compassion on the multitude, because they have now continued with Me three days and have nothing to eat. And I do not want to send them away hungry, lest they faint on the way'" (Matt. 15:32). The context is Christ's preparation to feed the four thousand who followed Him into the wilderness.

4. "So Jesus had compassion and touched their eyes. And immediately their eyes received sight, and they followed Him" (Matt. 20:34). The context is Christ's response to the two blind men who, as Jesus passed by, asked Him to heal them.
5. "Then Jesus, moved with compassion, stretched out His hand and touched him, and said to him, 'I am willing; be cleansed'" (Mark 1:41). The context is Jesus' response to the leper, whose healing authenticated who Christ was and caused multitudes to search for Him.
6. "And Jesus, when He came out, saw a great multitude and was moved with compassion for them, because they were like sheep not having a shepherd. So He began to teach them many things" (Mark 6:34). Mark described the situation noted in Matthew 14:14 prior to the feeding of the five thousand.
7. "I have compassion on the multitude, because they have now continued with Me three days and have nothing to eat" (Mark 8:2). Mark described the situation noted in Matthew 15:32 as Christ prepared to feed the four thousand.
8. "When the Lord saw her, He had compassion on her and said to her, 'Do not weep'" (Luke 7:13). The context is Christ's raising the son of a widow, a miracle that authenticated who He was.

The above accounts do not tell if tears were in His eyes. But they do tell us that Christ felt pity. Pity ought to motivate us to share Christ with the lost even if there are no tears in our eyes.

Paul displayed such pity for the lost condition of God's chosen people, the Jews. We read in Romans 9:1–3, "I tell the truth in Christ, I am not lying, my conscience also bearing me witness in the Holy Spirit, that I have great sorrow and continual grief in my heart. For I could wish that I myself were accursed from Christ for my brethren, my countrymen according to the flesh."

Paul anguished over the rejection of the gospel by a majority of the Jewish people. Were tears in Paul's eyes as he thought of their condition? We aren't told. The text emphasizes that he so pitied them that it brought "great sorrow" and "continual grief." Paul wished himself "accursed" or separated from Christ if it could secure their salvation. Such a sacrifice, of course, couldn't secure anyone's salvation. What Paul expressed is the pity he felt toward his own people who didn't know the Lord.

I don't subscribe to the philosophy that "big boys don't cry." I'm not ashamed to cry, but I don't cry as easily as some. I grieve inwardly more than outwardly. As one with the gift of evangelism, at times I lay awake at night, thinking of some person's eternal destiny if that person doesn't trust Christ. The pity is there even when tears aren't.

While I was waiting in the Chicago Midway airport for my return trip to Dallas, I noticed a cheerful woman across from me. She was wearing a lavender T-shirt that said, "Grandkids are from heaven." I complimented her shirt and, as we talked for a few moments, she told me that she was on her way to visit her grandkids in Alabama. Her eyes twinkled when she said, "I know they'll love my shirt." Airline personnel issued the boarding call for my flight, so I said, "I'm a speaker, and I'm in the ministry. I thought while you're waiting for your flight you might enjoy reading this tract." With that, I gave her one of our "May I Ask You a Question?" tracts (see Appendix) and boarded the plane. For days, I couldn't get her off my mind, wondering if she'd trusted the Savior. I thought of her several times a day, yet I never shed a tear.

What if a believer doesn't have such pity?

Ask God to give you pity for the lost. God encourages us to come to Him not only for physical needs, such as food and finances, but for any need we have. Hebrews 4:16 says, "Let us therefore come boldly to the throne of grace, that we may obtain mercy and find grace to help in time of need." When we come to Christ, our compassionate High Priest, we find comfort and help, not criticism and punishment. He is a God of mercy and grace. With a broken heart, ask Him, "Help me see lost people the way you see them." He *will* answer.

Read the gospel of John, a chapter a day, which explains how to receive eternal life. Imagine yourself by Jesus' side, and observe how He walked and acted around non-Christians. His concern for the lost can be instructive and contagious. When He talked with Nicodemus, for example—a man with religion but without Christ—He received his compliment, "Rabbi, we know that You are a teacher come from God; for no one can do those signs that You do unless God is with him" (John 3:2). Yet at the same time, Christ yearned for Nicodemus's conversion, not his compliments. His love poured through His alarm. "Most assuredly, I say to you, unless one is born again, he cannot see the kingdom of God" (v. 3). One chapter later, Christ crossed cultural and political lines and spoke to a Samaritan woman reprobate. What mattered were not her feelings about Him but His feelings about her. He explained, "If you knew the gift of God, and who it is who says to you, 'Give Me a drink,' you would have asked Him, and He would have given you living water" (John 4:10). Reading the gospel of John helps you see lost people the way Jesus did.

Spend time with unbelievers. Move out of your comfort zone. Spend time with those who are slaves of Satan and "dead in trespasses and sins" (Eph. 2:1). You'll realize Who you have and Who non-Christians don't have, and you'll long for them to understand: "Therefore if the Son makes you free, you shall be free indeed" (John 8:36). A woman attended a cocktail party sponsored by her husband's employer. As she mingled with the people he mingled with daily, she heard profanity used unsparingly. People spoke in a demeaning fashion; husbands and wives returned hateful and hurtful glances. She told me afterward, "My husband and I get so distressed for them. We keep trying to figure out how to reach them for the Lord. They're so unhappy and they don't even know why."

Spend time with those concerned for the lost. Let them "infuse" you. Let them "stir up love and good works" (Heb. 10:24) in this area. You may be surprised at how quickly their pity for the lost rubs off on you. Pity for the lost will not come overnight, but it will come.

Conclusion

The Bible doesn't teach that if you do not shed tears for the lost you'll not be effective in evangelism. Ask yourself, "Do I feel pity toward lost people who have not met the Savior?" If so, tears may or may not accompany such pity. If pity exists, though, one has the spirit that Christ had for lost people.

> **Tears don't determine effectiveness in evangelism. What matters is feeling pity for the lost.**

Misconception 9

"You're saved even if you're trusting something in addition to Christ for your eternal salvation."

((•))

An attorney—breast cancer at thirty-nine got her attention. She now took seriously what before she took lightly. She wanted to know she was going to heaven, and she now felt she had that assurance. So I asked, "What do you think you have to do to get to heaven?" Her answer was, "Love others and believe in Christ."

An engineer—his girlfriend got his attention. He and his attractive girlfriend attended church four out of five Sundays. He'd been going for a year and a half and referred to himself as a Christian. But I never assume anyone's salvation, so I gave him the "test" question. "If you stood before God and He were to ask you 'Why should I let you into heaven?' what would you tell Him?" His answer was, "I don't think He'll ask the question. He knows me. He knows how good I've been. Besides, I believe in Christ." So I said, "Let me ask another question. What do you think you have to do to get to heaven?" He answered, "Live a good life, keep the commandments, that sort of thing."

A factory worker—the tumor got his attention. I couldn't get our conversation out of my mind. Things didn't look good. He was awaiting the results of the biopsy, and he feared it was malignant. On top of that, he'd just been laid off at work. No job. Mounting bills. Nowhere else to go, he started to look up. He thought he'd better get right with

God. To him that meant to get baptized, and he was adamant. Jesus Christ was essential to get to heaven. So was baptism. Unless baptized, he assured me, he could not be saved. I asked, "Suppose a man died on his way to the baptismal pool. Where would he go?" He answered, "God would respect his heart. The man would have been baptized if he'd had time." But there was no question in his mind, Christ *and* baptism are necessary to be saved.

With testimonies like these, the formula for salvation is not the sufficiency of Christ. "Yes," those people would say, "Christ is needed. But salvation is through Christ *plus* any number of possibilities— baptism, church attendance, a good life, keeping the commandments, or taking the sacraments." Many people have said to me, "Don't you think they'll still get to heaven since they believe in Christ, even if they add something else to it?" One person said, "Christ is still part of their formula so they'd be okay, wouldn't they?"

Why is it a misconception to believe that people are saved even though they're not trusting Christ alone to save them?

The reasons are abundant. They're distinguishable, they're interrelated, and they're clear. Let's look at seven reasons—all biblical truths.

Eternal life is the appropriation of a gift, not the agreement to a partnership.

What distinguishes a gift? The price has been paid. If the receiver contributes to the cost, the gift isn't really a gift. Instead, it's a partnership in which two parties receive the benefit. If each does his or her part, they each profit.

Scripture never presents eternal life as the benefit of a partnership: if you do your part God will do His. Instead, it's the appropriation of a gift. Consider Ephesians 2:8–9 and Romans 6:23. Both passages attest to the gift of eternal life being imparted not *because* of human effort but *apart from* human effort.

Ephesians 2:8–9 says, "For by grace you have been saved through faith, and that not of yourselves; it is the gift of God, not of works, lest anyone should boast." Why does the text emphasize "that not of yourselves" and "not of works"? The refutation of both ideas is stunning. It is "not of yourselves" because "it is the gift of God." It is "not of works." The reason? "Lest anyone should boast." Both refute any thought of partnering with God. The bragging rights of salvation do not belong to two participants—the sinner and God. They belong to one—God. Human involvement in earning the gift is out of the question.

In Romans 6:23 we read, "For the wages of sin is death, but the gift of God is eternal life in Christ Jesus our Lord." Wages are earned. As sinners we've earned death and eternal separation from God. Apart from Christ, just one sin means hell is our future. What is placed in contrast to what is earned? The verse concludes, "But the gift of God is eternal life in Christ Jesus our Lord." Does sin earn us death? Yes. Does any amount of good living earn us eternal life? No. Romans 6:23 once again places the gift apart from any human effort.

God is not in debt to anyone.

Romans 4:5 reads, "But to him who does not work but believes on Him who justifies the ungodly, his faith is accounted for righteousness." One of the questions God will *not* ask us in determining if He should let us into heaven is, "How many good works have you done?" Why? Because righteousness is accorded "to him who does not work, but believes. . . ."

Why does God not accept human works as even partial payment of our salvation? Back up one verse to Romans 4:4: "Now to him who works, the wages are not counted as grace but as debt." If God accepted us based upon any good work we've done, any merit we've achieved, He would be paying a debt—giving something He owes. But God is not in debt to anyone. He doesn't owe us anything. Give us something? Yes. Owe us something? No.

Suppose you own a spacious mansion. It has marble floors, faux finished walls, a state of the art kitchen, granite countertops, high vaulted ceilings, tennis courts, and a pool inviting you into the beautifully landscaped backyard. I ask, "May I come live with you?" You respond, "Sure. All I ask is that you do these ten things." We strike a deal, and I do all ten. You're now my debtor. You owe me the right to live in your house. But God owes us nothing. He is not in debt to anyone. If we had anything to do with our salvation, that would make God a partial debtor.

That's why the Bible speaks of living a life of gratitude for our salvation. God owes nothing to us. We owe everything to Him.

Grace with any effort extended on our part is no longer grace.

Grace is favor we don't deserve. Actually, it's even more; grace is favor to those who deserve the opposite. As sinners, we deserve hell, but God gives us favor we don't deserve. He allowed His Son to take our punishment on a cross so that through His death and resurrection we could be forgiven. With the punishment paid, God gives favor to those who deserve the opposite. We deserve hell. His favor gives us heaven.

What happens if we add human effort to grace? Romans 11:6 explains, "And if by grace, then it is no longer of works; otherwise grace is no longer grace. But if it is of works, it is no longer grace; otherwise work is no longer work." Grace and works are diametrically opposed in our eternal salvation. Grace with any effort attached is no longer grace.

"It is finished" means it is finished.

The pain was brutal. Nails ripped through the ligaments in His wrists. Blood and sweat mingled on His forehead, stinging the puncture wounds from the crown of thorns. His feet throbbed as He attempted to support His weight. He could barely breathe. Most people laughed at Him, but He could also hear the cries of the few who loved Him. He knew they didn't understand what was happening. Through swollen eyes, Jesus caught a glimpse of His mother. He knew her heart was aching. His own side would soon be pierced with a sword. In His humanity, He wished for the suffering to be removed (Mark 14:36).

In His divinity, He knew He was "the Lamb of God who takes away the sin of the world" (John 1:29).

Finally, He could say from the cross, "It is finished" (John 19:30). And, indeed, His work on earth was done. The Greek word translated "finished" is *tetelestai.* Not only does it mean finished, it means paid in full. Receipts for taxes during New Testament times have been discovered with *tetelestai* written across them. Before an almighty God, Christ declared our sins paid in full. He didn't make the down payment; He made the full payment.

First John 2:2 tells us, "And He Himself is the propitiation for our sins, and not for ours only but also for the whole world." *Propitiation* means satisfaction. A holy God was satisfied with His Son's death as sufficient payment for our sins. Christ could declare, "It is finished" because the payment for our sin was complete.

The Cross shouts, "Be satisfied with the thing that satisfies God." If we're satisfied with good works as sufficient payment for our sins, we're lost and without eternal salvation. If we're satisfied with our good works *and* Christ's death, we're equally as lost. If we're satisfied with our baptisms as sufficient payment for our sins, we're lost and apart from God. If we're satisfied with our baptisms *and* Christ as payment for our sins, we're without Christ. God was satisfied with one thing only—His Son's death. A perfect person took the sinner's place. "It is finished" means the payment is complete. Nothing more can be added.

There is one gospel. It must not be perverted.

The gospel as declared in 1 Corinthians 15:3–4 is, Christ died for our sins and rose from the dead. Age, culture, and circumstances change nothing. The Good News is the same for the teen with many years ahead as it is for the dying man with moments to spare. It's the message America with its plenty or Africa with its poverty most needs. It's *the* gospel for the world. The people to whom it is spoken or the place in which it is spoken change nothing.

Paul's concern, or more likely righteous anger, as he wrote Galatians is understandable: "I marvel that you are turning away so soon from Him who called you in the grace of Christ, to a different gospel, which is not another; but there are some who trouble you and want to pervert the gospel of Christ" (Gal. 1:6–7). Those perverting the gospel of Christ were the Judaizers. They started by saying you had to believe in Christ to be saved but they didn't stop there. They added to that the keeping of Jewish feasts, circumcision, and keeping the ceremonial laws. All, they said, were requirements for salvation. Their gospel became not a gospel of grace but a gospel of grace plus works.

Paul warned, "But even if we, or an angel from heaven, preach any other gospel to you than what we have preached to you, let him be accursed" (Gal. 1:8). *Accursed* conveys the idea, "Let him suffer the discipline and displeasure of God." How God exercises that discipline is up to Him. For the non-Christian, the ultimate discipline is an eternal hell. For the Christian who distorts the gospel, God's discipline could be exercised in a variety of ways. Paul's point is that one who distorts the gospel deserves God's discipline. Why? A gospel of Christ *plus* was a different gospel. Paul says "which is not another," meaning another of the same kind. It's a different gospel, not another gospel of the same kind. Therefore it is not "Good News" at all.

There is but one God, one Savior, one gospel, one way of salvation. Peter declared, "Nor is there salvation in any other, for there is no other name under heaven given among men by which we must be saved" (Acts 4:12).

The clarity of John is unmistakable.

The purpose of the gospel of John, as emphasized repeatedly throughout this book, is to explain how to receive eternal life (John 20:31). Examine just three verses:

> For God so loved the world that He gave His only begotten Son, that whoever believes in Him should not perish but have everlasting life. For God did not send His Son into the world to condemn the world, but that the world through Him might be saved.

He who believes in Him is not condemned; but he who does not believe is condemned already, because he has not believed in the name of the only begotten Son of God. (John 3:16–18)

According to verse 16, the person who has eternal life is "whoever believes." According to verse 17, who is the one Person by which one must be saved? "Through Him," that is, God's only Son, Jesus Christ. According to verse 18, what is the basis upon which one is condemned or not condemned? Belief in the Son.

A student of Scripture might ask, what about John 3:5?—"Jesus answered, 'Most assuredly, I say to you, unless one is born of water and the Spirit, he cannot enter the kingdom of God.'" Doesn't "born of water" mean baptism? Three things must be noted. One is the context. Christ was attempting to take Nicodemus from the physical birth he had in mind to the second birth Christ had in mind. The context favors the view that the water Christ referred to is the water of physical birth. He was saying, "Unless one is born of water in order to live, and then of the Spirit to live forever, you cannot enter the kingdom of God." Second, drop down thirteen verses to John 3:16, which says that the one condition of salvation is faith in Christ. Third, the Scriptures do not contradict themselves. Therefore, regardless of how you understand water, Christ was not adding any requirement to His gift of eternal life other than faith. Since John repeatedly conditions salvation on faith alone, the clear must always interpret the unclear.

Christ's unmistakable words were, "Most assuredly, I say to you, he who believes in Me has everlasting life" (John 6:47).

Justification is based upon His Son's performance, not upon ours.

Justification is the act of God's grace by which those who believe are clothed with the righteousness of His Son and are declared 100 percent righteous in God's sight. On what basis is a sinner justified? Romans 5:1 explains, "Therefore, having been justified by faith, we have peace with God through our Lord Jesus Christ."

As we trust in Christ to save us, God no longer sees our sins. They have been covered by the blood shed on the cross. He so clothes us with His Son's righteousness that when God looks upon us, He only sees the perfection of His Son. We stand 100 percent righteous in His sight. The declaration is final. Upon faith in Christ we are eternally justified.

Romans 3:24 says we are "justified freely by His grace through the redemption that is in Christ Jesus." Freely means "without a cause." Our justification is based upon His Son's performance, not upon ours. There is no cause or merit within us to be justified.

Why do some struggle with a "Christ alone" salvation?

If one is saved through Christ alone, why do some say, "Well, my friend isn't trusting Christ alone, but I think he's still saved"? Grace and the gifts of God are hard for many to accept. We're accustomed to working for and earning everything we have—cash in the bank, the clothes on our backs, the burgers on our tables, the cars in our garages, the roofs over our heads. Haven't we been told God helps those who help themselves? Parents might help children get established, but the kids have to take it from there. A rich aunt might name you in her will, but that only covers some things, it won't pay for everything. When we're in dire straits, others may help out, but they can't bail us out completely. So when God says eternal life is free, it's almost too difficult to grasp. If "nothing in life is free," as we declare, how could eternal life be free?

Sometimes it's difficult to face the truth. If we admit to the truth of Scripture—that we're saved only through Christ alone—the ramifications can be enormous. That means an acquaintance who doesn't see the truth before he or she dies will be separated from God forever. The reality of what that means for our families, close friends, or neighbors is deeply emotional and personal. Avoiding the facts, though, doesn't change the facts. I may not like the truth, but the truth—not my feelings—needs to be preeminent. Wouldn't it be better to ask God for an opportunity to lead those people into the truth of the gospel?

We underestimate Satan's strategy. Satan is a deceiver. You won't recognize him by his dress or conduct. He might even wear the suit of a preacher. He'll probably encourage you to be as much like God as possible without being related to God. He's on the side of religion; he's not opposed to it, as long as the religion leaves out a Christ-alone salvation. That way, he can deceive people right into an eternal hell.

Salvation is often reduced to a formula. Just say or do this and you'll be right with God. Eternal life has nothing to do with a formula. It has everything to do with the appropriation of a gift. We come to God as sinners, recognizing that His Son took our punishment and rose again, and we trust His Son to save us. When reduced to a formula, we create our own ingredients for salvation. One ingredient is Christ, the other is whatever we determine it to be.

Conclusion

The Cross of Christ cries out, "Be satisfied with the thing that satisfies God." God was satisfied only with His Son's death as sufficient payment for our sins. That's why Christ declared, "It is finished." God is not in debt to anyone. He offers eternal life only on the basis of grace—favor we do not deserve. Grace with anything added to it ceases to be grace. God justifies us based upon His Son's performance, not ours. Should we trust in anything in addition to Christ for salvation, we've fallen victim to Satan's deception. Christ, and Christ alone, saves.

> **Be satisfied with the thing that satisfies God. If we trust in anything in addition to Christ as our only way to heaven, we haven't appropriated the free gift of eternal life.**

"If you doubt your salvation, then you're not saved."

$((\bullet))$

Doubt about her salvation plagued her. It felt like a nightmare from which she could not awake.

On two different occasions, she'd gone forward in a church service and was living for Christ. Yet from her teens into her married years, she just wasn't absolutely certain that she was going to heaven. Assurance of her salvation seemed elusive. It felt like trying to capture mountain air in a jar so she could smell it when she got home. Or like a baby trying to touch his shadow on the nursery wall against the angled afternoon sunlight. Or trying to catch a snowflake on her tongue. She could almost get it, but not quite.

Most people who voice doubt about their salvation fall into one of two categories. Some haven't understood the gospel and, indeed, are not saved. They think heaven is obtained through good works or a combination of Christ *and* their good works. If that were true, no one could be sure of his or her salvation; people, after all, may perform well one day and poorly the next. The Bible teaches that eternal life is free because the price for our sin has already been paid.

When I spoke at a friendship dinner, the associate pastor and his wife brought Jake and Ellen, a non-Christian couple. Jake asked if they could bring their friends Keith and Christina with them as well. The associate pastor said that would be fine. He knew Keith and Christina and had always assumed they were believers. That night Jake and Ellen trusted Christ . . . and so did Keith and Christina! Keith said to me,

"Had Jesus Christ asked me, 'Why should I let you into heaven?' I wouldn't have said, 'Jesus Christ died for me.' I've never understood this." He'd struggled with his salvation. Why? He had never understood the gospel. That night, the aroma of the gospel surpassed the aroma of the dinner. He finally understood!

The second category of people *have* understood the gospel. They're aware that the Bible doesn't speak of an "I hope so" or "I think so" salvation, but instead an "I know so." First John 5:13 asserts, "These things I have written to you who believe in the name of the Son of God, that you may know that you have eternal life." Yet these people still struggle with whether or not they're saved.

Herein lies the problem.

Since trusting Christ means eternal life is a certainty, not a possibility, some have maintained, "If you doubt your salvation, then you're not saved. After all, if you were saved, you'd *know* you are saved and know why."

Julia was as bright a teenager as I've ever met. Radiant face, upbeat personality, contagious laugh. She added zest to every situation. Yet she was not afraid to be transparent, real, authentic. When she told me of her doubts, I asked some critical questions. She gathered that she hadn't made herself clear. So she said, "Wait a minute. My problem is bigger than *why* I doubt my salvation. I've been told if you doubt *at all,* you're not saved. Is that true?"

Once again, many who doubt their salvation haven't understood the gospel. But dare we say that *everyone* who doubts his or her salvation is in that camp? Isn't it probable that Satan would torment God's children, getting them to wonder if they will, indeed, be in His presence forever?

What does the Bible say?

The Bible *guarantees* eternal life to a person who has trusted Christ. To assure us of our everlasting relationship with Him, the book of Romans affirms,

What then shall we say to these things? If God is for us, who can be against us? He who did not spare His own Son, but delivered Him up for us all, how shall He not with Him also freely give us all things? Who shall bring a charge against God's elect? It is God who justifies. Who is he who condemns? It is Christ who died, and furthermore is also risen, who is even at the right hand of God, who also makes intercession for us. Who shall separate us from the love of Christ? Shall tribulation, or distress, or persecution, or famine, or nakedness, or peril, or sword? (Rom. 8:31–35)

A second thing to note is that no verse teaches, "If you doubt your salvation then you're not saved." Such a statement is a misconception, not a biblical truth. Os Guinness, in his book *In Two Minds*, says, "There are three basic misconceptions which are especially common; first, that doubt is wrong because it is the same thing as unbelief; second, that doubt is a problem which troubles faith but not knowledge; and third, that doubt is something to be ashamed of because it is dishonest to believe if you have doubts."[1]

I agree with Os when he says people err in thinking that "doubt is wrong because it is the same thing as unbelief." Such teaching is not biblical. Change for a moment the word "doubt" to "question." I have more respect for those who question their salvation than for the person who doesn't question it at all. What greater question could one ask oneself than, "Am I sure I'm going to heaven and if so, why?"

Why, then, do people doubt?

Some people doubt everything. They doubt whether their mates love them, or whether their children respect them. They doubt that they'll reach the age of retirement, or that the plane they're taking will reach its destination. They're doubters at heart. Such people have issues they must deal with that are far different than eternal salvation.

Others doubt because they can't point to a specific time and place when they "crossed the line" and trusted Christ. They know that Christ alone is their only hope of salvation but if they don't know the exact moment they met their Savior, they wonder, "Could that mean I'm not saved?" They may have been told, "If you don't know the date you were saved, you're not saved" (see Misconception 1).

Others doubt because they've made the characteristics of a Christian the *conditions* upon which to determine if they are one. Someone e-mailed to me an article she wanted to submit to be published, asking for a critique beforehand. The subject was "How to Know If You Know Him." Turning to 1 John, the author suggested five questions to determine if one is saved:

1. Do I have fellowship with the Father?
2. Am I abiding in Him?
3. Do I practice sin habitually?
4. Do I love the brethren?
5. Am I overcoming?

How would these questions determine if I'm saved? One day I might respond affirmatively to one of those questions and another day I might respond negatively.

The purpose of 1 John isn't to discuss how to become a Christian; rather it discusses intimacy with Christ once you're saved. The gospel of John and the epistle of 1 John are great companion volumes. In his gospel, John tells how to receive the gift of eternal life, mentioning the word *believe* ninety-eight times. The book of 1 John discusses how to get close to the One you've trusted, using *abide* twenty-six times. Therefore, one's closeness to Christ is examined in 1 John, not one's salvation. With that in mind, 1 John 4:20–21 makes sense: "If someone says, 'I love God,' and hates his brother, he is a liar; for he who does not love his brother whom he has seen, how can he love God whom he has not seen? And this commandment we have from Him: that he who loves God must love his brother also." One can *know* God and hate one's brother. One cannot *love* God and hate one's brother. To be close to Him is to live in a right relationship with His family.

But sometimes the characteristics of an abiding Christian are presented as conditions for determining if one is a Christian. Looking at characteristics, though, can cause believers to doubt their salvation. Characteristics aren't conditions. Scripture points to people who didn't always display such characteristics, yet doesn't question their salvation. In 1 Corinthians 5, for example, Paul speaks of a person living in "such sexual immorality as is not even named among the Gentiles— that a man has his father's wife" (v. 1). Paul warns that the man may be judged with physical death, but assures his salvation is not in danger. He explains that the church is to "deliver such a one to Satan for the destruction of the flesh, that his spirit may be saved in the day of the Lord Jesus" (v. 5). The sexually immoral man needed church discipline, and believers were to break fellowship with him. Paul, though, refers to him as a "brother" (v. 11) and doesn't dispute his salvation.

People are often the victims of teaching that confuses entering the Christian life with living it. These people are also the ones who usually doubt their salvation. One who doesn't act like a Christian may not, indeed, be a Christian. But to use characteristics of a Christian as a basis for deciding whether one is a Christian isn't helpful. Some people might, after all, be living an exemplary life without being a Christian. It could be that those persons are trusting in their works instead of Christ's finished work on the cross to get them to heaven.

What should a doubter do?

How should doubts be handled? Keep in mind, these doubts *may* mean that a person isn't saved. Or doubts may mean that a person is saved but not responding to his or her doubts properly. The following questions help resolve the issue.

Do I understand the simplicity of the gospel?

Since we're accustomed to earning everything we have, we think in terms of earning salvation, or at least making a "down payment." When Christ died on the cross, He exclaimed, "It is finished" (John 19:30). His death and resurrection satisfied the anger of God against our sin.

He made the full payment, not the down payment, for everything wrong we have done. His resurrection the third day proved His victory over sin and the grave. Since He took the penalty of death in our place, God can now forgive us based entirely on what He has done for us. His forgiveness isn't based upon anything we've done for Him. As sinners we must recognize that He alone is the only basis upon which God can receive us.

Have I trusted Christ?

We appropriate Christ's death on the cross by coming to Him as sinners, recognizing that He made the sin payment on our behalf, and "believing." Jesus promised, "Most assuredly, I say to you, he who believes in Me has everlasting life" (John 6:47). *Believe* means to place our trust in Christ alone as our only basis for living eternally with God.

The issue is not *when* a person made such a decision, nor is it whether or not that person walked an aisle or said a prayer. Walking an aisle or saying a prayer may have happened in conjunction with coming to Christ, but those actions don't save. It is trusting Christ that saves. If we are trusting Christ alone to get to heaven, we are forever a child of God regardless of when or where that occurred.

If you're not certain you've trusted Christ, now is the time to settle that issue. Here's how you might verbalize to God what you are doing: *Dear God, I'm a sinner. Nothing I do makes me deserving of heaven. I now recognize that Christ died for me and rose again. Right now I place my trust in Christ alone to save me. Thank you for the free gift of eternal life that I have just received.* The moment you trust Christ, God freely extends the gift of eternal life.

Am I taking God at His Word?

Once we trust Christ, we must trust His Word. That means accepting God's promise that, having trusted Christ, we are forever His. Jesus assures us, "And I give them eternal life, and they shall never perish; neither shall anyone snatch them out of My hand" (John 10:28).

If you were to ask me whose son I am, I would respond, "I am the son of Paul and Miriam Moyer." I have proof that would stand up in a court of law—a birth certificate. A piece of paper assures me that I am their son. God has given us a piece of paper—the inspired Word of God. It assures us that once we've trusted Christ, we are His. Our salvation is based upon a promise that cannot be broken. It comes from a God who cannot lie.

When Satan tempts you to doubt, remember that Satan's argument is with God, not you. Refute Satan with the attitude, "If you want to argue about my salvation, you'll have to take your argument to my Savior. He said it and that settles it." Once Satan sees he can't torment you any longer, he'll flee and attempt to do his damage elsewhere. James's counsel, "Resist the devil and he will flee from you" (James 4:7), definitely applies.

Conclusion

The Scriptures do not teach that if you doubt your salvation you're not saved. If any person doubts his or her salvation, that person ought to ask the above questions and then take God at His Word. Should doubts arise, believers can recall that their salvation is as certain as the promises of God. When we respond properly to those doubts in a consistent way, questioning our salvation becomes a thing of the past. Those doubts may not fade overnight, but they will fade. Because of God's grace and promises, we can be 100 percent sure of heaven.

Doubting your salvation does not necessarily mean you aren't saved. Examine why you doubt and how to respond biblically.

"Living a Christlike life around non-Christians is enough. You really don't need to use words."

((•))

Ghandi, the former spiritual leader of India, was asked, "What is the greatest hindrance to Christianity in India?" He replied, "Christians."[1]

I knew a man who never missed an opportunity to say, "You really need to go to church." Yet he rarely went to church himself.

Few things damage the Christian witness more than a believer who doesn't live the life. Called "hypocrites," they talk much but appear unconcerned about how they live. The reverse is also true. Nothing *helps* the witness of a believer more than their life backing up their words. I've lead people to Christ who told of the influence other believers had in their lives. They say,

- "I know many who preach one thing and live another, but he lived the life he preached."
- "I thought he couldn't be the person he claimed to be because of what I had seen in other Christians. Was I ever in for a surprise."
- "Jesus Christ was as real to him on Monday as He was on Sunday."

The misconception that "a Christlike life is enough" has grown out of both negative and positive experiences. Sometimes it is captured by, "Just live your life around non-Christians. If necessary, use words," or "There's no need to speak to unbelievers about their need for Christ. Just live the life around them, and they'll come to the Savior." The idea is that if you live your day-to-day life you won't need to mention Christ to those around you; they'll ask you about Christ. But note what I've called it—a misconception.

Why is it a misconception?

We don't always excel in common sense. Imagine a woman who lives the Christian life perfectly (as if that were possible!). She puts others before herself, accepts insults without retaliation, and is a loving wife and mother. She controls her tongue instead of letting her tongue control her. She looks for ways to serve instead of looking for others to serve her.

Watch that woman for a day—or better yet, a week, a month, or a year. No amount of watching such a life tells me how to know Christ personally. If you live the holiest life, that merely verifies that something happened to you. It doesn't tell me how that same experience can be mine, or what causes you to live as you do. Maybe you're just a person of high morals. Perhaps your parents disciplined you well as a child.

Words are more than just helpful for me to know about Christ; they're essential. Sooner or later, someone has to talk to me about Him. That's not to say that a person can't come to Christ through the personal reading of Scripture. Some have, including me. Yet even in my own experience people said things that played a part in my understanding God's plan of salvation.

Yes, you need to live the life.

One passage stressing the importance of living the life is Matthew 5:14–16. We are told, "You are the light of the world. A city that is set on a hill cannot be hidden. Nor do they light a lamp and put it under a basket, but on a lampstand, and it gives light to all who are in the house. Let your light so shine before men, that they may see your good works and glorify your Father in heaven."

Contractors don't build a city on a hill to hide it. They want people to see it. In the same way, neither do you put lamps under baskets. The word *basket* here refers to a peck measure used for measuring corn. In the homes of that day it was a common piece of furniture. When not measuring corn it was turned upside down and used as a lamp stand. In that elevated position, the lamp lit the entire house. It allowed a mother to watch her toddler, and it allowed a toddler to find his toy.

Christ then makes His point. In verse 16 He says, "Let your light so shine before men, that they may see your good works and glorify your Father in heaven." Don't hide your Christianity. Take it with you to college. Practice it on the job. Display it in department stores. Let people see your good works. When a Christian does good, that believer points people to a God who is even better—"that they may see your good works and glorify your Father in heaven." Your light points people in the right direction and to the right Person.

Yes, you do need to use your lips.

A passage that stresses the importance of life *and* lips is Philippians 2:14–16. Paul urged the Philippians to do everything "without complaining and disputing." He then said, "... that you may become blameless and harmless, children of God without fault in the midst of a crooked and perverse generation, among whom you shine as lights in the world, holding fast the word of life."

Light here refers to heavenly bodies that illuminate the universe. What the sun is to the world, we are among non-Christians—a light in the midst of darkness.

How do we do this? In verse 16 Paul explains, "holding fast the word of life." That means to hold before nonbelievers the good news of Jesus Christ, which, as defined in 1 Corinthians 15:3–4, is the truth of Christ's death and resurrection. We are to evangelize. We must share the gospel at every opportunity, publicly to the masses and privately one on one. Acts 5:42 tells us, "Daily in the temple, and in every house, they did not cease teaching and preaching Jesus as the Christ."

Live the life. But also use your lips. Otherwise, nonbelievers will never know how to receive God's gift of eternal life.

What else does Scripture teach?

Although slightly different, another error is related to the misconception of "just live a Christlike life," and also fails to present accurately what Scripture teaches.

Often referred to as "friendship evangelism," the idea is that you must win the right to be heard. The comment made is, "If we do use words, we should know the lost person well before sharing Christ with that person."

We must be like Christ, who was a friend of sinners (Matt. 11:19). Sometimes, though, our best opportunities are our first conversations with the lost. The Samaritan woman of John 4 is a prime example. Christ's conversation with Zacchaeus in Luke 19 is another: "Make haste and come down, for today I must stay at your house" (v. 5). The text tells us that Christ led Zacchaeus to Himself during their first visit. That God-given opportunity sometimes results because God used someone else to sow the seed of the gospel but wants us to reap the fruit. After talking with the Samaritan woman, Christ told His disciples, "I sent you to reap that for which you have not labored; others have labored, and you have entered into their labors" (John 4:38). You do need a friendship, but some friendships are built in moments instead of months.

The teaching that says, "We should know the lost person well before sharing Christ with that person," fails to take into account the brevity of life. Two passages warn of that brevity in alarming tones. James 4:13–14 tells us, "Come now, you who say, 'Today or tomorrow we will go to such and such a city, spend a year there, buy and sell, and make a profit'; whereas you do not know what will happen tomorrow. For what is your life? It is even a vapor that appears for a little time and then vanishes away."

Those doing the boasting have decided everything—from when they are leaving to how much profit will be made. James reminds them that the only thing certain is that everything is uncertain. James describes their life as a "vapor that appears for a little time and then vanishes away." Here today, gone tomorrow has been a grim truth for too many. James explains, "You ought to say, 'If the Lord wills, we shall live and do this or that'" (v. 15).

The second passage is a parable that Christ told after sternly rebuking the disciples' covetousness. We read in Luke 12:16–20,

> Then He spoke a parable to them, saying: "The ground of a certain rich man yielded plentifully. And he thought within himself, saying, 'What shall I do, since I have no room to store my crops?' So he said, 'I will do this: I will pull down my barns and build greater, and there I will store all my crops and my goods. And I will say to my soul, "Soul, you have many goods laid up for many years; take your ease; eat, drink, and be merry."' But God said to him, 'Fool! This night your soul will be required of you; then whose will those things be which you have provided?'"

The rich man's four "I wills" reveal that this man is confident about the future. He is, in fact, planning for the future as though nothing could change it. God calls him a fool. The rich man put all his attention into the things that would be useless when he died. Knowing what the man did not know, God informed him that he didn't even have a full twenty-four hours. Death would come sooner than he thought.

Evangelism recognizes the brevity of life. In the case of some people, we don't have a hundred tomorrows to speak. We may not have one. To approach evangelism with a "whenever" attitude is not scriptural. Years ago I spoke at a friendship dinner in Michigan. A woman, who we'll call Kathy, invited a non-Christian couple, and they accepted the invitation but canceled three hours before the banquet. Kathy quickly invited another couple and the husband trusted Christ. Kathy and her husband attended our training seminar the next evening. They became convinced that they could talk to others about the Savior.

Days later, the wife of the couple who had canceled called Kathy. She had been in a car accident, rolled the car several times, and landed upside down in a ditch. She wasn't injured and walked away from the accident, but she told Kathy, "I truly thought I was going to die! I was so scared! What would have happened to my children if I would have died?"

Kathy responded, "More importantly, what would have happened to *you* if you'd died? If you died in that accident, can you tell me where you'd spend eternity?" Kathy then had the privilege of sharing the gospel with that woman and, amidst tears, the non-Christian trusted Christ. One week later, the woman collapsed in her home, was taken to the hospital, and died. Her death was caused by kidney failure from a disease she didn't know she had. Evangelism has to recognize the brevity of life. We aren't guaranteed tomorrow to speak to a lost person.

That's one reason I prefer the term "lifestyle" evangelism to friendship evangelism. Lifestyle says it. Every day is an outreach to non-Christians whom God brings across your path. You may not have the opportunity to present the gospel—but then again, you may. If you can't lead a person to Christ, just do as much as you can.

Conclusion

The idea that "all we need to do is live a Christlike life around non-Christians" is a misconception. If we aren't careful it becomes an excuse for not evangelizing. The most perfect life doesn't tell an unbeliever how to come to Christ. We must ask God for boldness to speak about the Lord.

As we do, we must realize how much more effective our witness is when backed up by consistent Christian living. The comment has been made, "Your life speaks so loudly I can't hear what you're saying." It's used of someone who seeks to witness for Christ but whose life leaves a lot to be desired. Such a life hinders our witness. It should be said of us, "I like what your life says. Please tell me more."

> **The holiest life doesn't explain how to receive eternal life. The Bible emphasizes our witness not apart from words, but accompanied by words.**

"Not all believers are expected to evangelize, just those gifted in evangelism."

((•))

Kristie was startled by Amy's response. Kristie hadn't meant to make her uncomfortable. As they lunched together, Kristie talked about the opportunity she'd had to share the gospel with a coworker the day before. Amy put down her fork, stared at her Caesar salad, then looked up and responded, "That's fine for you. But don't expect me to do it. Evangelism isn't something God expects all of us to do."

No one denies that evangelism is important, or even essential. The question is, "For whom is it essential?" Amy's opinion was that God doesn't expect every believer to evangelize. She believed He only expects those who are gifted in evangelism to share the Good News. To understand the flaw in Amy's logic, five questions need to be answered.

Where does such a view come from?

The Bible verse often cited to support such a view is Ephesians 4:11. We read, "And He Himself gave some to be apostles, some prophets, some evangelists, and some pastors and teachers." People interpret that to mean, "Since God has gifted certain people as evangelists, only those with that gift are expected to evangelize."

What is Ephesians 4:11 really saying?

Undeniably, this verse says God has gifted people within the church. Their purpose is stated one verse later: ". . . for the equipping of the saints for the work of ministry, for the edifying of the body of Christ." The goal is to equip believers so that together the work is accomplished. The responsibility God has given the church is not fulfilled by one person or even a few people. Instead, all believers are to use their spiritual gifts, and labor together. Who are these gifted people whom God has given to the church?

The apostles included the twelve disciples who were appointed by Christ (Acts 1:21–22). First Corinthians 15:8–9 indicates that Paul was also an apostle. Others had the gift of apostleship, although not the "office," because they carried the gospel message with God's authority. Among those were James (1 Cor. 15:7; Gal. 1:19), Barnabas (Acts 14:4, 14; 1 Cor. 9:6), and Andronicus and Junia (Rom. 16:7). Possibly included were Silas and Timothy (1 Thess. 1:1; 2:6) and Apollos (1 Cor. 4:6, 9).

Prophets revealed God's will to the church before the Scriptures were completed. Most Bible scholars teach that the apostles and prophets helped form the foundation of the early church, and that the gifts of apostleship and prophesy were no longer needed after the first generation of believers. Evangelists such as Philip (Acts 8:5, 26–40; 21:8) were to spread the gospel. Today, too, evangelists would be those who share the gospel with non-Christians at home and abroad. Pastors and teachers are listed together, and most scholars conclude that the terms refer to two functions of the same person. Pastoring is done by comfort and guidance; teaching is done through instruction in God's ways.

Thus Ephesians 4:11 teaches that specific people are given the gift of evangelism. As noted in a previous chapter, that gift could be defined as the special ability to communicate the gospel to sinners and to equip the saints for evangelism. Such people, then, have a gift and responsibility before the Lord to share the gospel and equip believers in evangelism.

Do *others* have the responsibility to evangelize?

Others *are* responsible to evangelize—for two reasons. One is within the text of Ephesians 4:11—the gift of evangelism is given "for the equipping of the saints." Ten or even ten thousand evangelists can reach only so many, so God wants evangelists to equip other believers to share the gospel. If they multiply themselves by equipping other believers, they can reach thousands, if not millions, more. A believer, then, doesn't have to have the *gift* of evangelism to evangelize. Believers can be equipped by someone with such a gift. Each year our association trains thousands in personal evangelism and evangelistic speaking, and those trained are going to places around the world.

The second reason is the nature of discipleship. Upon trusting Christ as our personal Savior, God invites us to be His disciples. Salvation is free and is given to us the moment we trust Christ. But discipleship involves a cost. Christ's caution in Luke 14:26 was, "If anyone comes to Me and does not hate his father and mother, wife and children, brothers and sisters, yes, and his own life also, he cannot be My disciple." Loyalty to Christ must come before loyalty to anyone else.

Disciple means "learner." In Matthew 4:19, we find the first thing Christ taught the first disciples when He called, "Follow Me, and I will make you fishers of men." If one is to be a disciple of Christ, one must in some way be involved in evangelism. Concern for lost people should characterize a disciple of Christ.

That concern may be expressed in various ways. Some give financially, and their monetary investments bring spiritual dividends—the lost are reached. Other believers may promote an evangelistic outreach by helping orchestrate an event that proclaims the gospel to hundreds, even thousands. Still others may distribute evangelistic literature, thereby proclaiming the gospel through the printed page. Those who pray for evangelistic workers are also greatly needed. As some speak to people about God, those who pray speak to God about people. The point is, disciples of Christ must be involved in evangelism in some way.

In light of the biblical evidence indicating otherwise, why would anyone deny the need to be involved in evangelism?

Why, then, would a person say, "Not all believers are expected to evangelize—just those gifted in evangelism"? One reason, again, is a misapplication of Ephesians 4:11. Experience has taught me, though, that there's a more prominent reason. Many feel guilty for not evangelizing and are fearful of doing it. They attempt to ease their conscience by saying, "God doesn't expect all of us to evangelize." But wouldn't it be more honoring to God to face what hinders us in evangelism and learn to evangelize? When believers learn how to share Christ with clarity and boldness, evangelism is a desire, not a demand. Instead of a bitter pill, it becomes chocolate mousse! With proper training, we can look forward to opportunities to evangelize instead of dreading them.

Aren't there other reasons to evangelize?

If someone says, "God doesn't expect all of us to evangelize," that person ought to ask four common sense questions.

1. *What if the person who shared the gospel with me had thought "God doesn't expect me to evangelize"?* If we feel no need to approach people about their eternal destiny, would we have wanted the people who led us to Christ to have had the same attitude?
2. *If eternal life is the greatest gift, why not pass it on to others?* Suppose someone gave you a million dollars. The giver then says that anyone you know can receive that same gift. Wouldn't you feel compelled to tell others? How can we *not* tell people how they too can receive the greatest gift imaginable—eternal life?
3. *What is the only thing I can take with me to heaven?* The answer is a friend or acquaintance—whether it be someone we've known for thirty minutes or thirty years. Why not take as many friends

as possible so that those who are friends on earth will be friends for eternity? If we don't tell them how they can be with us in heaven, we should question the depth of our concern for them.

4. *Can I claim to be growing as a Christian if I don't desire to see people saved?* When we become close to someone, what that person is enthusiastic about rubs off on us. I never had a desire to water ski. I, in fact, had a paralyzing fear of water. A good friend was so enthusiastic about it, though, I started to think I was missing out on something. It became like a Mercedes I'd never driven, a best friend I hadn't met. I had to overcome my fear and learn to water ski. My friend's excitement was contagious!

Are we really growing close to Christ if what excites Him does not excite us? Christ's heart is for the lost. Luke 19:10 says, "For the Son of Man has come to seek and to save that which was lost." Mark 10:45 reads, "For even the Son of Man did not come to be served, but to serve, and to give His life a ransom for many."

Conclusion

The idea that not all believers are expected to evangelize—just those gifted in evangelism—is a misconception. Those with the gift of evangelism are to equip others so that the entire body of Christ can be involved in reaching the lost. Introducing others to Christ is part of discipleship. Getting close to the heart of Christ and following after Him means we must be involved in evangelism in some way. In addition to the biblical injunction to evangelize, there are other reasons. We are to do unto others as we would have them do unto us. If we're grateful that people reached out to us with the gospel, we ought to reach out to others. As we learn how to do so, we increase our skills and overcome fear in evangelism.

> **Christians who wish to be Christ's disciples must in some way be involved in evangelism.**

Misconception 13

"Unless you're willing to turn from your sins, you can't be saved."

$((\bullet))$

The argument goes like this:

"To come to Christ, you must do an about-face. You were headed one direction and must now head another. You must forsake the wrong things you used to do and cling to a new way of life. Without turning around, you are not sincere, and therefore will not be saved."

When we come to Christ, God wants us to live the holiest life we can for the Savior. First Peter 1:14–16 says, "As obedient children, not conforming yourselves to the former lusts, as in your ignorance; but as He who called you is holy, you also be holy in all your conduct, because it is written, 'Be holy, for I am holy.'" Our goal each day, then, should be to live a holy life, turning from all that displeases Him *to* all that pleases Him.

Having to turn from our sins, though, isn't a requirement for salvation. To claim it is confuses *entering* the Christian life with *living* the Christian life.

Where does such a misconception arise?

This misconception arises from two sources. The first is a wrong understanding of repentance. It's mistakenly defined as "turning from sin." One Scripture cited is 1 Thessalonians 1:9: "For they themselves declare concerning us what manner of entry we had to you, and how you turned to God from idols to serve the living and true God." Although the word *repentance* is not used in the verse, the passage is viewed as a picture of repentance. Repentance is consequently defined as a turning—a change of direction. This passage, though, is describing the conversion of pagan Gentiles. They worshiped gods who were not alive and not worthy objects of praise. For their salvation, they needed to place their faith in the one and only true God. Yes, they had to turn from their sin, but that sin related to the object of their worship not to the direction their life was heading. Their false gods could not save them. Only Christ could.

Repentance, used in a salvation context, means to change your mind about whatever is keeping you from trusting Christ, and to trust Him to save you. Standing on Mars Hill, Paul declared, "Truly, these times of ignorance God overlooked, but now commands all men everywhere to repent, because He has appointed a day on which He will judge the world in righteousness by the Man whom He has ordained. He has given assurance of this to all by raising Him from the dead" (Acts 17:30–31). What did Paul's listeners need to repent of? They had to repent of their erroneous concept of Christ and trust Him alone for their salvation.

Particular sins are mentioned in reference to repentance, but the context is who the people were and who they worshiped. They wouldn't admit they were sinners nor was Christ the object of their faith. In Revelation 9:20–21 we read,

> But the rest of mankind, who were not killed by these plagues, did not repent of the works of their hands, that they should not worship demons, and idols of gold, silver, brass, stone, and wood, which can neither see nor hear nor walk. And they did not repent of their murders or their sorceries or their sexual immoralities or their thefts.

The purpose, again, of the book of John is to tell us how to receive eternal life (John 20:31). We are told ninety-eight times to believe. Not once are we told to repent. Why? To believe, as John used it, is to repent. We come to God as sinners, recognize that Christ died for us and arose, and trust in Christ alone to save us. When we place our trust in Christ, both repentance and faith have taken place.

The issue is admitting we are sinners, not turning from our sins. Turning from sin is the *fruit* of repentance, not the *condition* of salvation. Turning from sins demonstrates our desire to follow Christ. We should "bear fruits worthy of repentance" (Matt. 3:8), but turning from sin is not a biblical prerequisite for salvation.

The second source of the misconception is a misuse of particular passages of Scripture. John 8 tells of a woman caught in an adulterous relationship. Christ's words to her were, "Neither do I condemn you; go and sin no more" (v. 11). Some ask, "Doesn't that require her to 'turn from her sins' if she is to come to Christ?"

The context, though, is critical. The scribes and Pharisees set themselves up as God's spiritual representatives to administer divine justice. They brought the guilty party to Christ, and no doubt they threw her down in the gritty sand in front of Him. The hurt, embarrassment, and shame she felt must have been humiliating. Instead of rebuking her for her sin, He rebuked them for theirs. He implored, "He who is without sin among you, let him throw a stone at her first" (v. 7). He caused them to face two things. First, to be His spiritual representatives they had to be without sin. Of course, they weren't. The second thing He caused them to face was that, with God, sin is sin. Christ did not say, "He who is without adultery. . . ." He said "He who is without sin. . . ." God's standard is perfection. The people who lie are as guilty before God as the people who lie in bed with someone other than their mates. "Being convicted by their conscience" (v. 9), the woman's accusers left.

Christ alone had the right to administer divine justice. His message to her was comforting, not condemning: "Neither do I condemn you; go and sin no more." Moments earlier she was an outcast with no friends. Now her enemies didn't matter. Moments earlier she faced death. Now she had reason to dance. We can hope that she did turn from her sin, but the context focuses on who Christ is, and what He did *not* do (condemn her). Christ didn't condition His acceptance of her upon whether she'd ever again commit adultery.

A second passage used as support for this misconception is the story of Zacchaeus in Luke 19. Zacchaeus used his profession of collecting taxes to overcharge the people and keep the extra for himself. Stolen coins jingled in his money pouch, but he acknowledged his wrong as he said, "Look, Lord, I give half of my goods to the poor; and if I have taken anything from anyone by false accusation, I restore fourfold" (v. 8). In the Old Testament, if someone stole one item, that person had to return four times what had been taken. To steal one sheep demanded four in return (cf. Exod. 22:1). Zacchaeus admitted his sinful condition.

Upon that acknowledgment Christ exclaimed, "Today salvation has come to this house, because he also is a son of Abraham" (v. 9). Why? Christ continued, "for the Son of Man has come to seek and to save that which was lost" (v. 10). Numerous commentators agree that the interaction between Christ and Zacchaeus described in verses 9 and 10 took place in Zacchaeus's home *after* he had placed his faith in Christ. We would hope he never cheated a person again, but we don't know that for sure. The text doesn't tell us. We're told only that Christ acknowledged Zacchaeus's admittance of his sinful and lost condition. Zacchaeus personified the people Christ came to save—the lost. The passage is not meant to emphasize what Zacchaeus had to do but who Christ came to save—sinners. One cannot come to Christ as a good, moral, religious person. He must come the way Zacchaeus came—as a sinner.

I spoke with a young woman on an airplane returning from Florida. She told me that she'd recently met a man through the Internet, and he flew her to Florida where they could begin a relationship. When she arrived, he said that he no longer cared for her and sent her back home. I asked, "Where do you work?" She answered, "It's hard to find a job when you're pregnant." It turns out that a man in Pennsylvania had gotten her pregnant. As I presented the gospel, she told me she wasn't interested in Jesus. Her reason? She'd asked Him to do a number of things for her, such as healing her uncle's cancer. The uncle died. To her, Christ was a disappointment and a failure. She saw many ways that Christ had failed her, yet she saw no way that she'd failed Him. Despite her sin, in her mind she was quite "righteous." Until people see themselves as lost, they will not see their need of Christ.

What is the problem with the "turn from your sin" exhortation?

The "turn from your sin" exhortation calls upon non-Christians to do what they're incapable of doing. Paul described every lost person's condition:

> . . . you once walked according to the course of this world, according to the prince of the power of the air, the spirit who now works in the sons of disobedience, among whom also we all once conducted ourselves in the lusts of our flesh, fulfilling the desires of the flesh and of the mind, and were by nature children of wrath, just as the others. (Eph. 2:2–3)

We were children and slaves of Satan. He owned and directed us. Only when indwelt by the Spirit of God can we say *no* to Satan and *yes* to God. That's what gives significance to Christ's words in John 8:36: "Therefore if the Son makes you free, you shall be free indeed." Our relationship with Christ frees us from the dominion of Satan and the power of sin over our lives. In the Amish part of Lancaster County, Pennsylvania, you see many horse-drawn carts. The expression, "Don't put the cart before the horse" has visual meaning there. The horse is the power that drives the cart. The cart can't drive the horse. In the same way, only the power that brought Jesus Christ up from the grave can, as it indwells us, enable us to turn from our sin. That power is ours upon and after conversion, not prior to conversion.

The second problem with the "turn from your sin" exhortation is that it overlooks a most basic requirement. We must see ourselves as sinners who deserve to be separated from God. Where, how, and when we turn from those sins only matters *after* coming to Christ. Even the Pharisees turned from sin. They proudly confessed, in fact, that they were not like other men. The Pharisee of Luke 18 confessed, "God, I thank You that I am not like other men—extortioners, unjust, adulterers, or even as this tax collector" (v. 11). The Pharisee also made certain God knew what he *did* do: "I fast twice a week; I give tithes of all that I possess" (v. 12). It's unfortunate, though, that he didn't see himself as a sinner. The same paragraph also tells of a tax collector acknowledging his sinful condition: "And the tax collector, standing afar off, would not so much as raise his eyes to heaven, but beat his breast, saying, 'God, be merciful to me a sinner'" (v. 13). It can be hoped that he never again used his occupation as a tax collector to cheat people, but we're not told. We are told, though, that he admitted his sinful condition. Christ declared, "I tell you, this man went down to his house justified rather than the other; for everyone who exalts himself will be humbled, and he who humbles himself will be exalted" (v. 14). The issue for salvation is acknowledging we are sinners, not when and how we turn from that sin.

The third problem with "turn from your sin" is that this exhortation ignores the gospel of John. When answering the question "What must one do to come to Christ?" the first place we should turn is to the gospel of John (see John 20:31). The lost person is asked to come to God as a sinner, to recognize that Christ died for him or her and arose, and trust in Christ alone for salvation. Upon coming to Christ, God will help us turn from those things that are sinful and destructive. The gospel of John emphasizes who we are—sinners—and what we must do—believe. Trust in Christ alone to save. The emphasis is who we are and Who we come to, not what we turn from.

A fourth problem relates to our integrity. Suppose we say to the lost, "Unless you turn from your sin you can't be saved." Have we turned from ours? We must not maximize the sins of others and minimize our own. I'm often asked, "How do you witness to a homosexual?" My answer is, "The same way you witness to anyone else. You explain that we all are sinners, Christ died for us and arose, and we have to trust Christ." The sin of homosexuality may be offensive to us, yet unkind thoughts, selfish attitudes, lying tongues, and overeating are also offensive to God. I'm often tempted to say, "Why didn't you ask me, 'How do you witness to a person with a quick temper? How do you witness to someone who's selfish?'" To God, sin is sin. Any sin is an abomination in His sight. When we tell others that unless they turn from sin they can't be saved, we're

Pharisaic and judgmental. We enforce standards upon others that we don't enforce upon ourselves.

There's yet another problem with "turn from your sin"—one I alluded to earlier. It confuses entering the Christian life with living it. Upon coming to Christ, what are we exhorted to do? Grow! Second Peter 3:18 says, "Grow in the grace and knowledge of our Lord and Savior Jesus Christ." How do we grow? We grow through the Word. Second Timothy 3:16–17 explains, "All Scripture is given by inspiration of God, and is profitable for doctrine, for reproof, for correction, for instruction in righteousness, that the man of God may be complete, thoroughly equipped for every good work." Through the Word, God shows us what to take out of our lives that displeases Him, and He shows us what to put in. Through time and study, we live and grow as Christians "turning from our sins." First we enter the Christian life, then we live it. Don't confuse the two.

What do the Scriptures exhort us to do?

First, we must come to Him as sinners. The issue is not how we feel about our sin, it's how God feels about sin. The issue is not, are we willing to turn from sin? The issue is, are we willing to admit that it is sin in God's sight, worthy of eternal condemnation?

Suppose that a certain man is unwilling to come to Christ because he's *afraid* of what God might do with the sins he's enjoyed. If that man so enjoys his immorality or overeating and, in fear of what God might do, is unwilling to come to Christ, he needs to examine Mark 9:43–48: "If your hand causes you to sin, cut it off. It is better for you to enter into life maimed, rather than having two hands, to go to hell, into the fire that shall never be quenched—where 'Their worm does not die and the fire is not quenched.'" Mark uses the same terminology as he speaks about the foot and the eye. Nothing is worth going to hell over. What our hand touches, where our foot takes us, or what our eyes see—does it keep us from coming to Christ? We'd be wise to cut off the hand, cut off the foot, and pluck out the eye. It's better to be here with one than separated from God with two.

But how do we know if people are sincere or just want "fire insurance"? Not wanting to go to hell is, actually, an excellent reason for coming to Christ. It is the reason I came. I didn't understand victorious living or the need to live a life of gratitude for my salvation. I had no knowledge of the indwelling presence of the Holy Spirit. I just didn't want to go to a horrible fiery hell. I was comforted to know that I wouldn't if I came to Christ. As sinners who deserve to be eternally damned for our sin, not wanting to go to hell is a proper reason for coming to Christ. Nowhere in Scripture are we asked to test people's sincerity. If people are insincere, they're only fooling themselves. They're the ones who lose.

In most cases, when people are labeled insincere because they don't follow through with growing in Christ, the fault rarely lies with them. It's likely that such people didn't know what they were doing. The gospel wasn't presented clearly or follow-up was nonexistent. They may well have trusted Christ, but had little encouragement to grow or instruction in how. Lacking follow-up, new converts may never understand that they can not only escape hell but also experience abundant living as a part of knowing Christ.

Secondly, upon recognizing we are sinners, we must trust in Christ alone as our only way to heaven. He paid for those sins by dying as our substitute and rising the third day. Our trust cannot be in Christ *and* the changed life we plan to live. We must trust Christ alone as our only way to eternal life. Salvation is not on the basis of Christ plus, but Christ period.

Lastly, once we trust Christ we must then recognize that the Christian life is not a natural life. It's a supernatural life. We will struggle with sin. Paul said in Romans 7:18–19, "For I know that in me (that is, in my flesh) nothing good dwells; for to will is present with me, but how to perform what is good I do not find. For the good that I will to do, I do not do; but the evil I will not to do, that I practice." We can turn from sin one day and be tempted by it the next. In our own power, our temptation will be to do wrong, not to do right.

We don't live the Christian life—instead, Christ lives it through us. Paul said in Galatians 2:20, "I have been crucified with Christ; it is no longer I who live, but Christ lives in me; and the life which I now live in the flesh I live by faith in the Son of God, who loved me and gave Himself for me." As we depend upon the Holy Spirit who indwells us, we have the power to live the life He intended us to live. Galatians 5 testifies to the fruit of the Holy Spirit, not the *human* spirit: "But the fruit of the Spirit is love, joy, peace, longsuffering, kindness, goodness, faithfulness, gentleness, self-control" (vv. 22–23). His Spirit empowers us to live a life characterized by righteousness and not dominated by sin.

Conclusion

In coming to Christ, we must see ourselves as sinners and recognize Him as our only Savior. As people held captive by Satan, we must rely upon Christ alone—not our self help, sincere promises, or steps of reformation—to free us from those sins. Only through His shed blood in our place can we be delivered from the eternal damnation we deserve. Upon trusting Christ, by His help we can live a new life in which we "turn from our sins." We can live a life that, before conversion and the appropriation of His power, we had no ability to live.

> **God doesn't ask us to turn from sin to be saved. He asks us to call ourselves sinners and trust Christ to save us. Then He helps us to turn from what displeases Him and to live the holiest life we can.**

Misconception 14

"If you don't love your brother or sister in Christ, then you're not saved."

((•))

Something weighed her down. I knew her to be a genuine, sincere person—not afraid to admit her weaknesses. Yet the creases in her forehead betrayed the calm demeanor she tried to display. Then she shared what troubled her. "Sometimes I don't love people the way I should or the way others do—even the people in my church. Does that mean I might just *think* I'm a Christian and not be one?"

Ask people, "What should be the predominant quality characterizing most Christians?" Almost without exception they say "love." We ought to love others because He loved us.

What if we don't? Does that mean that we're not Christians? On the basis of two Scripture passages, some argue, "Yes, that means that person is not a Christian."

What does Scripture say?

Two passages are used to support the thought that if we don't love our brothers or sisters in Christ, we're not saved. Both are located in 1 John.

1 John 4:7–8

First John 4:7–8 reads, "Beloved, let us love one another, for love is of God; and everyone who loves is born of God and knows God. He who does not love does not know God, for God is love."

It's essential to interpret Scripture in context. These verses are found in 1 John, not the gospel of John. Why does that make a difference? As I've stressed throughout this book, the gospel of John was written to tell us *how* to obtain eternal life. John says, "These are written that you may believe that Jesus is the Christ, the Son of God, and that believing you may have life in His name" (John 20:31). John tells us that we obtain eternal life by believing—trusting Christ alone to save us. Nowhere in the gospel of John is loving others a condition of salvation.

First John, though, was written to tell us how to get close to the One we have believed on—how to have fellowship with Him. John's purpose in writing this small epistle is found in 1 John 1:3–4: "That which we have seen and heard we declare to you, that you also may have fellowship with us; and truly our fellowship is with the Father and with His Son Jesus Christ. And these things we write to you that your joy may be full." Remember, John used the word *believe* ninety-eight times in his gospel. He used the word *abide* twenty-six times in 1 John, explaining how to have fellowship with Him. We know Christ by believing, we get close to Christ by abiding—by walking with Him daily and depending upon Him to live His life through us.

God's nature is loving—"Love is of God; everyone who loves is born of God and knows God" (1 John 4:7). Scripture uses two different words for *know*. One means "to know something as a fact"; for example, facts tell you who your parents are. The other means "to know by experience"—having lived with your parents, you know them on a deeper level. The word *know* in this portion of 1 John means to know Him through the experience of walking with Him.

What if we aren't loving? The next verse reads, "He who does not love does not know God." John isn't saying such a person doesn't know Him as Savior, he's saying that person doesn't have a close walk with

Him. If she did have a close walk, and since God is love, she would be a loving person.

With that in mind, note what John says four verses later: "If we love one another, God abides in us, and His love has been perfected in us." In 1 John, the issue of loving others is not whether we've trusted Christ. It's whether we are *abiding* in Christ.

1 John 4:20–21

In 1 John 4:20–21 we read, "If someone says, 'I love God,' and hates his brother, he is a liar; for he who does not love his brother whom he has seen, how can he love God whom he has not seen? And this commandment we have from Him: that he who loves God must love his brother also."

When we understand the context of 1 John, these verses also become clear. The text does *not* say "If someone says 'I believe in Christ,' and hates his brother, he is a liar." It says, "If someone says 'I *love* God' and hates his brother, he is a liar." You can be related to God and hate your brother. How many Christians struggle in that area? Do you? You can't *love* God and hate your brother. As 1 John 4:21 says, "He who loves God must love his brother also." So if you love the Father, you have to love the family.

It is not a person's *relationship* with God that 1 John addresses. It's that person's *closeness* with God. God doesn't give eternal life with stipulations attached. So you may have trusted Christ and still hate your brother. One cannot love God, though, and hate one's brother. To love Him is to love His family.

Love is a requirement of discipleship.

Once we trust Christ, God invites us to be His disciples. Again, a disciple is a "learner"—someone who follows after Christ and learns more about Him. Although salvation is free, discipleship can be costly. To those who would be His disciples, Christ warned, "If anyone comes to Me and does not hate his father and mother, wife and children, brothers and sisters, yes, and his own life also, he cannot be My disciple. And whoever does not bear his cross and come after Me cannot be My disciple" (Luke 14:26–27).

What did Christ desire of those who would be His disciples? In John 13:34–35, He says, "A new commandment I give to you, that you love one another; as I have loved you, that you also love one another. By this all will know that you are My disciples, if you have love for one another." Two chapters later, He repeated the same exhortation: "These things I command you, that you love one another" (John 15:17).

Christ removed all boundaries. He took love to an extent that our human nature would not take it. He said, "You have heard that it was said, 'You shall love your neighbor and hate your enemy.' But I say to you, love your enemies, bless those who curse you, do good to those who hate you, and pray for those who spitefully use you and persecute you" (Matt. 5:43–44). The reason? It's easy to love the people who love us. It takes discipleship to love those who hate us. Christ continued, "For if you love those who love you, what reward have you? Do not even the tax collectors do the same? And if you greet your brethren only, what do you do more than others? Do not even the tax collectors do so?" (vv. 46–47). Someone has said, "To love a friend is natural. To love an enemy is Christlike."

Without abiding in His love we cannot love others. If we're not loving others, we're not walking in obedience as disciples. Love is the issue for discipleship, not salvation.

Not only do we have His power to do what we ourselves cannot do, we also have His example. Scriptures show how loving and forgiving Christ is. We understand His depth of love when He took our punishment on a cross. If He could so love us, how can we *not* love others? As 1 John says, "Beloved, if God so loved us, we also ought to love one another" (1 John 4:11).

Years ago, when the Lord's Supper was being celebrated in a little mission church in New Zealand, a dramatic thing happened. Worshipers knelt at the altar. Knees were bent and heads were bowed. The air was still. Suddenly, a young man stood and marched back to his seat. His face and posture revealed his anger. Yet, a few moments later, he reverently returned to the altar to partake of communion. Afterward a friend asked what all the going back and forth was about. He said, "When I first knelt I found myself next to the man who killed my father years ago. He'd spilled my father's blood, and I vowed to kill him in revenge. As I drank from the cup and saw the dark red wine reminding me of the Savior's blood, I just couldn't partake with that murderer next to me, especially knowing the hatred in my own heart. So I returned to my pew. But as I sat there, I pictured the Upper Room, with its table set. The wine and the bread were laid out. The bitter herbs, the lamb, all were spread before me in my mind. Then I heard a voice say 'By this all men will know that you are my disciples, if you have love for one another.' Then I saw a cross with a man nailed to it. Blood poured down and mixed with the sand below. The same voice said, 'Father, forgive them, for they know not what they do.' It was then I arose and returned to the altar."[1]

Conclusion

"If you don't love your brother or sister in Christ, then you're not saved" is a misconception. Loving others is not a result of simply coming to Christ but a result of *abiding* in Christ. Love, then, is a requirement of discipleship. As we abide in Him, we have His ability to love others—even our enemies—as He has loved us. When we do, we represent to the world that we are His disciples.

> **Loving our brother or sister in Christ is not a condition of salvation. It is the result of close communion with Christ and following Him.**

Misconception 15

"If you come to Me, I'll make you both healthy and wealthy."

$((\bullet))$

It's called the "health and wealth" gospel. It's encouraged people to pray for anything from a Lexus to a lake house. The exhortations are specific. If you need a thousand dollars, ask God for a thousand dollars. If you need five thousand, ask Him for five thousand. If you'd like a successful stock portfolio, ask Him for a successful stock portfolio. One preacher said, "You tell God what He needs to do for you."

The thought goes like this: "God doesn't want His children to live in poverty or sickness. That's the Devil's plan, not God's. Now that you're a Christian, you can say to the Devil, 'Get thee behind me, Satan. I'm not going to be sick or poor anymore.'" As a result, the "health and wealth" gospel has even been used to rebuke those with a terminal disease: "If you had enough faith, you wouldn't be lying there sick and dying."

Proponents teach that if we are children of the King we should live like children of a king. We have a divine right to "name it and claim it," so just tell God what you expect, then watch it happen. Sickness and poverty are not God's will for His children, so if you don't have both health and wealth, you may not have come to Christ at all.

The way Scripture has been mishandled in developing this misconception is alarming.

What biblical support do such people use?

Although several passages are used to support such teaching, five are used most.

Deuteronomy 8:18

And you shall remember the LORD your God, for it is He who gives you power to get wealth, that He may establish His covenant which He swore to your fathers, as it is this day.

The Lord gives you "power to get wealth." So if you're not experiencing financial prosperity, it's claimed, there's something spiritually wrong.

The passage, though, is a warning, not a promise. In verses 14–16, God reminds the people of four things that He did for them. He brought them out of Egypt, led them through the wilderness, provided water from a rock, and fed them with manna in the wilderness. Each provision was a test to see if they would depend upon the Lord. Would they recognize God's gifts or credit their own ability? The temptation was to say, "My power and the might of my hand have gained me this wealth" (v. 17). Failure to praise Him would lead to forgetting Him. Forgetting Him would lead to worshiping other gods. Such worship would result in their destruction, as it had the destruction of other nations. The chapter concludes, "Then it shall be, if you by any means forget the LORD your God, and follow other gods, and serve them and worship them, I testify against you this day that you shall surely perish. As the nations which the LORD destroys before you, so you shall perish" (vv. 19–20).

The text doesn't promise prosperity. It warns of the danger of not crediting God for any prosperity that one experiences.

Ecclesiastes 11:1

Cast your bread upon the waters, for you will find it after many days.

It is said, "Give what you have to the Lord. He will return many times over what you gave." Specifically used of financial prosperity, the idea is you can't outgive God. He will return to you more than you gave Him.

The context explains the intended meaning. One verse later we read, "Give a serving to seven, and also to eight, for you do not know what evil will be on the earth." One never knows what disaster one might face, and this verse is an exhortation to prudent investing. "Cast your bread upon the waters, for you will find it after many days" means, "Send your grain across the seas and in time you will get a return." "Give a serving to seven, and also to eight" means, "Don't put all your eggs in one basket." Instead, make prudent investments in numerous ventures.

The paragraph speaks to the fact that investment in business promises some return. But we are not told how great that return will be. Some investments turn out better than others. This passage is about work and prudence, not the promise of prosperity.

Malachi 3:10

> "Bring all the tithes into the storehouse, that there may be food in My house, and try Me now in this," says the LORD of hosts, "if I will not open for you the windows of heaven and pour out for you such blessing that there will not be room enough to receive it."

The argument is, give to God and watch what He gives back to you. If you give to Him, you'll experience material prosperity. Your gifts to Him are seeds that reap a crop of abundance.

These verses, though, are in the context of a special covenant relationship that God had with Israel. The Mosaic Law of Deuteronomy 28 specified blessings for obedience and curses for disobedience. Israel is the only nation with whom God entered into such a covenant.

God had rebuked them for withholding their tithes and offerings, and they experienced His curses. God then begged them to return to

Him (3:7). How were they to return? What specific actions were they to take? They were to "bring all the tithes into the storehouse." *Storehouse* refers to a room or rooms in the temple where tithed grain was stored (cf. Neh. 10:38; 13:12). God would consequently bless them with agricultural prosperity, and they could count on fertile fields and rich harvests. One verse later, God tells them that their crops would not be destroyed by pests, that their verdant vines would be undamaged. In addition, they would have a good reputation among the nations (Mal. 3:12). The only thing preventing such blessing was their lack of obedience to His commands. Again, the Malachi promise is set in the context of the Mosaic covenant to Israel. Hebrews 8:13 teaches that God has made a new covenant with us, but nowhere in Scripture is any nation told that God will deal with them on the same basis as He did with Israel.

Does God promise to meet the needs of those who meet the needs of His people? Yes. Philippians 4:19 encourages us, "And my God shall supply all your need according to His riches in glory by Christ Jesus." As the Philippians met the needs of the gospel ministry (by their gift to Paul), God in turn met their needs. The Philippians passage, though, is not a blanket promise that with our gifts to God comes physical and financial prosperity. Remember, God promises to meet *needs*, not wants.

John 15:7

> If you abide in Me, and My words abide in you, you will ask what you desire, and it shall be done for you.

Capitalizing on the phrase "ask what you desire," the idea is given that if you state what you wish, you will have it—"it shall be done for you." The application is made, if you want a new home or a new car, more money or a better job, just ask. It will be yours.

This verse, though, is talking about abiding in Christ. Only as we depend upon Him are we fruitful. Look two verses earlier, where we read, "I am the vine, you are the branches. He who abides in Me, and I in him, bears much fruit; for without Me you can do nothing." We are to so abide in Him that our wills are conformed to His, that we want only what He wants for us. With that kind of conformity to His will, the prayers of our lips match the desires of His heart. Since our desire equals His, we can ask what we desire and it shall be done for us.

In addition, this passage is talking about spiritual fruit, not physical provisions. The next verse reads, "By this My Father is glorified, that you bear much fruit; so you will be My disciples" (v. 8).

Contrary to being a "name it and claim it" verse, John 15:7 urges conformity to God's will. There are more important things than physical and financial prosperity. When our hearts are close to His, our wills and wants match His. We desire to be spiritually fruitful. We can then ask what we wish, knowing it will be done.

3 John 2

> Beloved, I pray that you may prosper in all things and be in health, just as your soul prospers.

Some would ask, "What could be a clearer wish for good health and prosperity?" As the "soul prospers," we are increasingly Christlike, with a goal to live the holiest life possible for Christ. Therefore, God desires our physical health to be the same. Some would argue that the phrase "you may prosper in all things" includes the financial arena as well.

Third John, though, is a personal letter to Gaius (v. 1), and John's purpose was to encourage him to show hospitality to Demetrius (v. 12), a traveling preacher who was also the bearer of John's letter. Verses two through six demonstrate Gaius's authentic spirituality, and it was John's wish that Gaius get along just as well on the physical level. So the apostle's concern for both Gaius's temporal and spiritual well-being was obvious. Verse two could, in fact, be paraphrased, "I hope that both spiritually *and* physically you do well."

Such a greeting encourages us to pray not only for the spiritual needs of others, but for their temporal needs as well. To carry the thought any further is not warranted by the text. No mention of finances is made.

Also, had Gaius suffered illness, which undoubtedly at times he did, John would have prayed for his health. Nothing suggests, though, that he would have said to him, "If you had more faith, you wouldn't be sick."

Many believers mentioned in Scripture did not profit physically or materially.

Believers, then, are not promised health or wealth. Some of God's greatest servants did not, in fact, experience earthly prosperity. Yet their conversion is not questioned nor is it associated with their physical circumstances.

Consider the book of James.

James's book was written to those undergoing trials. They were separated from loved ones, and had lost their possessions. Living in a time of life-threatening persecution, they were scattered throughout the Roman Empire. James wrote to tell them how to endure trials and live the Christian life amidst difficult conditions. He wrote, "Count it all joy when you fall into various trials, knowing that the testing of your faith produces patience" (James 1:2–3). James reminded them that their hope was in the Lord's return, not a change in circumstances. We read, "Therefore be patient, brethren, until the coming of the Lord" (5:7).

Consider the apostle Paul.

Paul was such an example of Christlikeness that he could say, "Imitate me, just as I also imitate Christ" (1 Cor. 11:1). Yet at times his health failed and his finances were scarce.

Whatever physical ailment he had (many believe it related to his eyes), he asked God to remove it three times. Each request was declined. He said, "And lest I should be exalted above measure by the abundance of the revelations, a thorn in the flesh was given to me, a messenger of Satan to buffet me, lest I be exalted above measure. Concerning this thing I pleaded with the Lord three times that it might depart from me" (2 Cor. 12:7–8). Paul received his answer, not in the form of healing, but strength to bear the ailment. The Lord's words were, "My grace is sufficient for you, for My strength is made perfect in weakness" (v. 9). With that assurance, Paul could say, "Therefore I take pleasure in infirmities, in reproaches, in needs, in persecutions, in distresses, for Christ's sake. For when I am weak, then I am strong" (v. 10).

In addition, Paul experienced times of great lack, not great prosperity. But he wanted more of Christ, but not more materially. He was grateful, for example, for the gift the church at Philippi extended to him, but he reminded them that they ministered to his need, not to his contentment. He said, "I know how to be abased, and I know how to abound. Everywhere and in all things I have learned both to be full and to be hungry, both to abound and to suffer need. I can do all things through Christ who strengthens me" (Phil. 4:12–13).

Although a person of deep spiritual devotion, Paul did not experience uninterrupted health and physical strength, nor did he gain wealth.

Consider the heroes of the faith.

Hebrews 11 lists heroes of the faith whose lives were characterized by sickness, need, and suffering, not "health and wealth."

> [They] were tortured, not accepting deliverance, that they might obtain a better resurrection. Still others had trial of mockings and scourgings, yes, and of chains and imprisonment. They were stoned, they were sawn in two, were tempted, were slain with the sword. They wandered about in sheepskins and goatskins, being destitute, afflicted, tormented—of whom the world was not worthy. (Heb. 11:35–38)

Scriptures warn against craving physical prosperity.

The believer is to live a life of contentment, not covetousness. Two paragraphs, one from Proverbs and one from 1 Timothy, discuss the proper attitude.

Proverbs 30:7–8 reads, "Two things I request of You (Deprive me not before I die): Remove falsehood and lies far from me; Give me neither poverty nor riches—Feed me with the food allotted to me." The writer recognizes the frailty of man and requests help in areas of his greatest weakness. One is protection from lying, and the other is provision of daily bread. In asking that his daily needs be met, he's aware of the temptations of wealth and poverty. Wealth could cause him to forget God and become a "self-made" man, poverty could cause him to forget God's character and become a thief. He asks, then, that he might be content with daily provision.

In 1 Timothy 6:6–10 Paul emphasized that would-be shepherds of the flock like Timothy have a need for contentment:

> Now godliness with contentment is great gain. For we brought nothing into this world, and it is certain we can carry nothing out. And having food and clothing, with these we shall be content. But those who desire to be rich fall into temptation and a snare, and into many foolish and harmful lusts which drown men in destruction and perdition. For the love of money is a root of all kinds of evil, for which some have strayed from the faith in their greediness, and pierced themselves through with many sorrows.

Why contentment? Because we leave the world the same as we entered it—carrying nothing in, carrying nothing out. Paul doesn't condemn money, but the *love* of money. When it comes to worldly possessions, the issue is contentment, not covetousness. We need to be satisfied with what we have, not crave more. It's not necessarily wrong to desire more materially, as long as we honor God with it. It's wrong when the desire for material prosperity overrides all else.

Believers should focus on what they have in the world to come, not on what they have in the present world.

We shouldn't focus upon where we live now or upon circumstances that we're living with. Scripture focuses instead on where we will live *then* and *Who* we will live with. In John 14, for example, the disciples were grieved that Christ was leaving them. Christ's comfort was, "Let not your heart be troubled; you believe in God, believe also in Me. In My Father's house are many mansions; if it were not so, I would have told you. I go to prepare a place for you" (vv. 1–2). What will make heaven spectacular? We will be where Christ is. In verse three, He continues, "And if I go and prepare a place for you, I will come again and receive you to Myself; that where I am, there you may be also." Heaven is paradise because Christ Himself is there.

We are citizens there, in fact, and "pilgrims" here (1 Peter 2:11). So we are to focus on the spiritual not the material, on the things lasting, not the things temporary. Paul says, "If then you were raised with Christ, seek those things which are above, where Christ is, sitting at the right hand of God. Set your mind on things above, not on things on the earth" (Col. 3:1–2).

We have no right to demand anything of God.

God is awesome, all powerful, supreme. No one is above Him. Everyone answers or will answer to Him. A day is coming "that at the name of Jesus every knee should bow, of those in heaven, and of those on earth, and of those under the earth, and that every tongue should confess that Jesus Christ is Lord, to the glory of God the Father" (Phil. 2:10–11).

We deserve nothing good from His hand. His mercy, in fact, protects us from what we do deserve, and His grace gives us what we don't deserve. Broken, we ought to ask, "What is man that You are mindful of him?" (Ps. 8:4). Our breath, energy, town homes, jobs, SUVs, friends, money, and food are all tokens of His goodness. We deserve nothing. We owe Him everything.

Never in Scripture do properly-minded believers *demand* anything of God. They may struggle with His ways. Habakkuk did. He questioned, "How can a just God use a wicked nation like Babylon to punish His chosen people?" In Scripture, too, some asked God for healing. Paul did. He prayed for Epaphroditus's healing. He said, "For indeed he was sick almost unto death; but God had mercy on him, and not only on him but on me also, lest I should have sorrow upon sorrow" (Phil. 2:27).

Is it okay to ask God for physical provisions? Yes. Christ, in fact, encouraged it when He taught His own disciples to pray, "Give us this day our daily bread" (Matt. 6:11). But we can't demand anything of God. We can expect good things of a good God, but we mustn't have the attitude of "telling God what He must do." Our attitude must be that of undeserving children making requests of a kind father. Anything less disrespects His holiness, and it shows a denial of our unworthiness.

Conclusion

Scripture never links the gospel to health or financial prosperity. One can trust Christ and be destitute financially or dying of spinal meningitis in a hospital room. As believers, our hope is not in what we have or hope to have in this life. Such hope is, at best, uncertain (see 1 Tim. 6:17). Our hope is in what we are promised in the life to come.

> **God doesn't promise His children health or wealth. Scripture speaks of who we are in Christ and what we can look forward to in the life to come.**

"If you come to Me, I want either all of your life or none of it."

$((\bullet))$

Either—or. All or nothing.

Some say, "You can't meet God halfway. If you want to come to Christ [that is, trust Christ as your Savior], you must completely surrender to Him. God will only do business with you if you mean business with Him. If you don't give Him all of your life, He doesn't want *any* of your life."

On the surface that appears to make sense, doesn't it? But what's the problem with that teaching? Why is it a misconception?

What passages are used to support such a teaching?

Three passages are commonly used, but their intended meaning is made clear by their context.

Matthew 6:24

> No one can serve two masters; for either he will hate the one and love the other, or else he will be loyal to the one and despise the other.

When used to argue for the misconception, the verse is often dropped there—but it continues: "You cannot serve God and mammon." The verse is not about salvation; Jesus was preparing to speak about worry. Since money is considered a "cure all" for worry, Jesus warned of the danger of letting money be one's master. The message is delivered in the context of truths in regard to those who would follow Him as disciples. In following Christ, one has to serve God. One cannot serve money.

Mark 10:17–22

> Now as He was going out on the road, one came running, knelt before Him, and asked Him, "Good Teacher, what shall I do that I may inherit eternal life?" So Jesus said to him, "Why do you call Me good? No one is good but One, that is, God. You know the commandments: 'Do not commit adultery,' 'Do not murder,' 'Do not steal,' 'Do not bear false witness,' 'Do not defraud,' 'Honor your father and your mother.'" And he answered and said to Him, "Teacher, all these things I have kept from my youth." Then Jesus, looking at him, loved him, and said to him, "One thing you lack: Go your way, sell whatever you have and give to the poor, and you will have treasure in heaven; and come, take up the cross, and follow Me." But he was sad at this word, and went away sorrowful, for he had great possessions.

The rich young ruler's question was to the point: "What shall I do that I may inherit eternal life?" Christ's answer was just as pointed. Not many things obstructed this man's path to inheriting eternal life— only one. But to the rich young man, that one thing amounted to giving up everything: "Go your way, sell *whatever* you have" (emphasis added).

Look at the young man's question, "What shall I do that I may inherit eternal life?" The word *inherit* in Jewish literature conveys the thought that to obtain eternal life, one had to meet certain conditions. But prior to His confrontation with the rich young ruler, Jesus had emphasized, "Whosoever does not receive the kingdom of God as a little child will by no means enter it" (v. 15). Another common Jewish thought at the time was, "Whom the Lord loves, He makes rich," riches being viewed as an indication of divine favor. To discover that his riches would not merit entrance into heaven was disconcerting to the young man. Jesus said to His disciples, "How hard it is for those who have riches to enter the kingdom of God" (v. 23).

Jesus knew the young man's heart. If the love for riches was enough to keep him from entering heaven, it would also prevent him from following Christ should he become a believer. To shake him out of his self-righteousness and show him his wrong attitude, Christ gave a compelling call to discipleship: "Go your way, sell whatever you have and give to the poor, and you will have treasure in heaven; and come, take up the cross, and follow Me." Grieved, the young man walked away.

Far from teaching that if we come to Christ, He wants all of our lives or none of our lives, the passage addresses this particular young man's struggle with priorities. He needed to depend upon Christ, not his riches, to get him to heaven. The same riches that kept him from Christ would have hindered him from becoming a disciple if he were a Christian.

Luke 14:26–27

> If anyone comes to Me and does not hate his father and mother, wife and children, brothers and sisters, yes, and his own life also, he cannot be My disciple. And whoever does not bear his cross and come after Me cannot be My disciple.

To be Christ's disciple, one must give up ownership of one's life. Love for Christ must be so strong that love for all others, including self, seems like hate in comparison. We must be willing to endure ridicule, hardship, and—if necessary—death for the cause of Christ. Christ's words left no room for compromise: "Whoever does not bear his cross and come after Me *cannot* be My disciple" (emphasis added).

Notice that the word *disciple* is used twice in Luke 14:26–27. Christ was speaking of discipleship, not of salvation. *Disciple*, remember, means "learner."

God wants us to come to Him as sinners, recognizing Christ died for us and arose, and trust in Him alone to save us. The moment we trust Christ we are His forever. His promise is, "Most assuredly, I say to you, he who hears My word and believes in Him who sent Me has everlasting life, and shall not come into judgment, but has passed from death into life" (John 5:24). We who are His children are invited to be disciples, to follow after Him and learn more about Him. Salvation is as simple as receiving a gift; discipleship involves a cost.

Jesus gave two illustrations about that cost—one about the cost of building a tower and another about the cost of declaring war. Christ explained, "For which of you, intending to build a tower, does not sit down first and count the cost, whether he has enough to finish it. . . . Or what king, going to make war against another king, does not sit down first and consider whether he is able with ten thousand to meet him who comes against him with twenty thousand?" (Luke 14:28, 31). The point is, "If you are going to be My disciple, you'd better count the cost."

To be disciples, we must give Christ complete control to do as He pleases. Again, discipleship is in view, not salvation—the two are not synonymous. Salvation is free; discipleship involves a cost. Yet reward is promised. Christ assured His disciples, "And whoever gives one of these little ones only a cup of cold water in the name of a disciple, assuredly, I say to you, he shall by no means lose his reward" (Matt. 10:42).

A misunderstanding of these verses is not the only problem. Truths are overlooked that are at the heart of the salvation message.

The means of salvation focus upon Christ's past performance, not our present or future performance.

Why do many miss the simple message of salvation? They work hard to earn everything they have, so they think they have to work to earn salvation too. That makes both their present and future performance critical. They believe the good they do must outweigh the bad, or they won't receive eternal life.

The means of our salvation focuses on Christ, not me; His performance, not mine; what has happened, not what will happen. Instead of our focusing on what He wishes we'd do for Him, Christ yearns that we understand what He has already done for us. The gospel focuses upon what He did—He paid for our sin. How? He, a perfect person, took our place, and that sacrifice was sufficient to pay for all sins of all people for all time. So I'm not saved through the life I give to Him but through His life that He gave for me. As He died in our place, Christ could declare, "It is finished" (John 19:30). The sacrifice of His life was, in fact, so complete that Hebrews 10:12 tells us, "But this Man, after He had offered one sacrifice for sins forever, sat down at the right hand of God."

Our salvation involves receiving a gift, not bargaining with God.

God does not extend the gift of salvation with conditions attached. Salvation doesn't occur on the auction block with God saying, "If I do this for you, what will you do for Me?" Rather, salvation is what Scripture calls a gift. In Ephesians 2:8–9 we are told, "For by grace you have been saved through faith, and that not of yourselves; it is the gift of God, not of works, lest anyone should boast." Christ is not saying, "I'll only do this for you if you do this for Me." God says, "Look what I've done for you. My Son died as your substitute and rose again. He shed His blood in your place. May I give you the gift of eternal life purchased by that blood?"

A gift isn't a gift if I have to earn it; it's only a gift if no strings are attached. Therefore, we're not saved on the basis of Christ plus our good life, we're saved by Christ alone. One is not justified before God when one bargains with God. We're justified only when we trust Christ alone to save us.

My wife, Tammy, and I headed to Boston for vacation. But the plane was overbooked and we couldn't sit together. We were placed a few rows apart, but that was God's appointment. The man next to me, a sociable person, couldn't wait to talk. Learning that I was in the ministry, he told me that he taught seventh graders in one of the largest evangelical churches in Dallas. I don't remember how we got into it, but soon I was explaining God's simple plan of salvation. He was amazed and enthusiastic. I asked if he'd understood that before, and he responded, "I always heard that Christ died for us, but I never understood that you have to trust Him *alone* for salvation." His understanding was that he had to bargain with God to be saved, and he thought that maybe if he taught youth at church, then God would let him into heaven. There, 35,000 feet above sea level, that man trusted Christ. Afterward, he said how grateful he was that God allowed our seats to be together. We exchanged addresses so I could send him a booklet on how to grow as a Christian. The gospel message is so simple yet millions miss it. Salvation involves receiving a gift already paid for, not bargaining with God.

The giving of my life is a response out of gratitude for Christ giving His.

Can one come to Christ with reservations about surrendering one's all to Him? Definitely. Recognizing that we're sinners who need salvation is the issue, not the surrender of our lives. Shortly before His crucifixion, Christ prayed, "Oh My Father, if it is possible, let this cup pass from Me; nevertheless, not as I will, but as You will" (Matt. 26:39). Christ surrendered to God's will, and His surrender to God secures our salvation, not our surrender to Him.

Anyone who has trusted Christ should want to please Him. So we ought to be willing to surrender our lives for however God desires to use it. But "giving one's all" is part of growth and discipleship. It is not a condition of salvation. The sacrifice of my life is a response to the sacrifice of His. In Romans 1–11, Paul explained that Jews and Gentiles alike received, through faith, the greatest gift there is—Christ's imputed righteousness. That allows us to stand 100 percent righteous before God. With that in mind, Paul exhorted in Romans 12:1–2, "I beseech you therefore, brethren, by the mercies of God, that you present your bodies a living sacrifice, holy, acceptable to God, which is your reasonable service. And do not be conformed to this world, but be transformed by the renewing of your mind, that you may prove what is that good and acceptable and perfect will of God."

In contrast to the sacrifices of the Old Testament, which were slain, we are to be living sacrifices, set apart and pleasing to God. Instead of being conformed to the world, each of us needs to be conformed to His will. My mind is to be so transformed that He controls my attitudes, thoughts, and actions. When that happens, I discover the "good and acceptable and perfect will of God." My surrender to Him is the most enjoyable and productive way I could live.

Although trusting Christ in my early teens, I wasn't surrendered to Him until years later. You may laugh at my reason, but for me it was serious. I love the outdoors and especially sports like hunting. God, in fact, used the outdoors to bring me to Christ. As I pondered nature, I knew there had to be a God. Why was the male pheasant's head so vividly colored red, black, and green, but the female's head was a soft brown? I marveled at the intricacy of an upturned clod of dirt, the rough, curvy bark on a tree, the white stars blinking against the black velvet sky. I compared the delicate speed of a deer to the plodding pace of a turtle and wondered at God's creation. Why did He create squirrels to climb trees to hide, but create rabbits to run and hide in the bush at the base of the same tree? I loved the fresh smell of rain as it hung in the air after a thunderstorm. I watched the shallow creek that meandered through our property. The clear water from the spring in the woods was so pure and cold, it was a most refreshing drink. As I pondered what I saw, I was impressed. But I was also empty. So I began to study the Bible and I came to Christ through that study. Yes, God took me from the creation to the Creator, to Christ.

Although I knew I'd be with Him forever, I wasn't certain at that point that I wanted to give my entire life to Him. I viewed surrender as all pain and no fun. I didn't think He'd let me enjoy anything exciting. The truth is, I didn't think He'd let me hunt anymore. I was afraid He'd take away the one thing I loved so much. After all, weren't surrender and sacrifice synonymous? So I tried bargaining with God.

He got ten months out of twelve, I got two—the length of hunting season. That sounded more than fair.

One night in Bible college I listened to a tape that sang of discipleship. I still remember the words:

> Jesus use me,
> And O Lord don't refuse me.
> For surely there's a work that I can do;
> And even tho' it's humble,
> Help my will to crumble,
> Tho' the cost be great,
> I'll work for you.[1]

I had always loved the melody but had ignored the message. By this point I had been a Christian a number of years, and I understood what Christ had done for me. But that night as I contemplated those words, it was as though Jesus Christ was face to face with me. I sensed Him saying, "Larry, the problem with you is that, when it comes to following Me, it's just talk." That night I said, "Lord, my life is yours completely." That night was the start of the greatest adventure I've ever known. It involves more fun than I ever knew it could. Any sacrifice has been worth it. I've gained, not lost. But I'm grateful that when He saved me, it was as a person not ready to surrender my all to Him. The moment I trusted Christ to save me, He gave me eternal life based upon His life, not based upon mine. Years later I discovered the joy of surrender.

The giving of one's life is a response to the giving of His. It's not a requirement of salvation; it's a response to salvation. Should such surrender not exist, eternal life is still ours. The unsurrendered believer, though, misses the present joy and future reward found in a life surrendered to God. Surrender is my way of saying to Him, "In light of what You have done for me in giving Your life, I want to express my thanks by giving mine."

Conclusion

Does God want all of our lives? Yes, He wants our discipleship after conversion. But He doesn't extend salvation on the basis of a promise that we make to God. He extends it *solely* on the basis of a provision He made for us. That provision was Christ's death on a cross, and His death secured our eternal life. As sinners, we are accepted by God based upon not what we plan to do with our lives, but upon what Christ did with His life.

> **Surrendering one's life to Him is an issue of discipleship, not salvation. We are accepted by God on the basis of what Christ did on the cross as our substitute, not what we plan to do with our lives.**

"Since I, God, am sovereign and will save whomever I choose, I don't need your help."

((•))

He spoke without reservation. "The thing that keeps me from evangelism is that I strongly believe in what the Bible calls election. God is going to save whomever He wills and He doesn't need my help."

Is God sovereign? Does "election by God" (1 Thess. 1:4) mean that He doesn't need our assistance in evangelism?

Using the scriptural teaching on election as an excuse to not evangelize is unbiblical. Two facts bear each other out: first, yes, God is sovereign; second, He has not only predetermined the end, He has also determined the means.

God is sovereign.

One of the strongest passages on God's sovereignty in our salvation is Ephesians 1:3–5:

> Blessed be the God and Father of our Lord Jesus Christ, who has blessed us with every spiritual blessing in the heavenly places in Christ, just as He chose us in Him before the foundation of the world, that we should be holy and without blame before Him in love, having predestined us to adoption as sons by Jesus Christ to Himself, according to the good pleasure of His will.

The two phrases "having predestined us to adoption as sons" and "according to the good pleasure of His will" give the unmistakable picture that God is, indeed, in control.

Just as clear are Paul's words to the church in Thessalonica when he expressed his gratitude to God for their salvation and encouraged them to "walk worthy of God who calls you into His own kingdom and glory" (1 Thess. 2:12). Paul's words were conclusive—God chose them.

With God's sovereignty stressed, the Bible also speaks of those who are elect. Paul admonished the believers in Colossae, "Therefore, as the elect of God, holy and beloved, put on tender mercies, kindness, humility, meekness, longsuffering" (Col. 3:12).

God, then, is sovereign, and the Bible's emphasis on predestination and election is undeniable. Upon what do both rest? Romans 8:28–30 points to His foreknowledge:

> And we know that all things work together for good to those who love God, to those who are the called according to His purpose. For whom He foreknew, He also predestined to be conformed to the image of His Son, that He might be the firstborn among many brethren. Moreover whom He predestined, these He also called; whom He called, these He also justified; and whom He justified, these He also glorified.

Foreknew means to know beforehand. What did God know in advance? Some argue that He knew who would trust Christ and who wouldn't and, consequently, chose them to be saved. That, though, is not what Scripture says. Furthermore, if *who would or wouldn't trust Christ* was the emphasis of "foreknew" it could be argued that man, not God, is in control.

Until we see Him face to face, we won't know everything meant by "whom He foreknew." (For a more complete discussion of this subject, the reader is referred to the author's book *Free and Clear,* Kregel Publications, 1997.) We do know that what He foreknew had a relationship to His choosing. The chosen are those "whom He foreknew" and are elected to be His children forever.

In evangelism, it's a comfort to know that God is in control. Should the person we speak to not trust Christ, that person's lost condition is not our responsibility. God is, ultimately, in control.

Does God's sovereignty negate man's responsibility to trust Christ? No. Several passages offer evidence, but one will do. In John 3:17–18, we read, "For God did not send His Son into the world to condemn the world, but that the world through Him might be saved. He who believes in Him is not condemned; but he who does not believe is condemned already, because he has not believed in the name of the only begotten Son of God."

Why is a lost person condemned? "Because he has not believed in the name of the only begotten Son of God," meaning that person rejected Christ. Yes, God is sovereign, but each person is still responsible; we can receive or reject God's offer of eternal life. To many, the notion of God's sovereignty and personal free will sounds at odds. But the Bible is often called a book of "harmonious opposites." Two things may appear opposite but are actually in harmony. That's true of the sovereignty of God and personal free will. God is sovereign and has elected some to be with Him forever, but each person is still responsible and must receive God's offer of eternal life. Although the sovereignty of God and the free will of man appear to be opposite to us, they are harmonious in the sight of God. When we see Him face to face, that harmony will be apparent. We'll see things from His perspective, not man's.

God has not only predetermined the end, He has also predetermined the means.

How do the elect hear the good news of the Savior? People are God's messengers. Examine Romans 10:14–15, 16–17:

> How then shall they call on Him in whom they have not believed? And how shall they believe in Him of whom they have not heard? And how shall they hear without a preacher? And how shall they preach unless they are sent? . . . But they have

not all obeyed the gospel. For Isaiah says, "Lord, who has believed our report?" So then faith comes by hearing, and hearing by the word of God.

Belief is based upon hearing, but how can someone hear if no one preaches? God's method is people reaching people. If an exception could be found in Scripture, it would be in Acts 9, the conversion of Paul on the road to Damascus. Even there, it could be argued that since Acts 9:1 tells us Saul was "breathing threats and murder against the disciples of the Lord," he could have heard the message from those disciples. Why else would he be persecuting them? With rare exception, then, the way God reaches people is through other people.

God could send angels to spread the Good News, or He could use His own voice to proclaim the gospel to the whole world. He is, after all, God, and has that ability. He could have chosen any way He wished, but He chose people reaching people.

God's decision to use people, in fact, is among the first and last things that Christ taught. The first thing Christ taught His disciples was, "Follow Me, and I will make you fishers of men" (Matt. 4:19). They knew how to scale a smelly fish; they didn't know how to fish for men. If they followed Christ, He promised to teach them everything they needed to know to bring people to Him. One of the last things Christ said to His disciples is commonly referred to as the Great Commission: "Go therefore and make disciples of all the nations, baptizing them in the name of the Father and of the Son and of the Holy Spirit, teaching them to observe all things that I have commanded you; and lo, I am with you always, even to the end of the age" (Matt. 28:19–20). They were to reach the lost and disciple them to reach others. They were to go from the sandy lake shores to the small villages to the big cities.

God, then, foreordained the means—people reaching people—not just the end. But many ways are used to achieve that end. It may be done through assisting in an evangelistic outreach, distribution of a tract, a song, one-to-one witnessing, or proclaiming the gospel to a mass audience. But God has foreordained that people reach people.

The following fanciful fable clearly illustrates God's plan: When Jesus ascended to heaven after His mission on earth, the angels asked, "Did You accomplish Your task?" The Lord answered, "Yes, it is all finished. I paid for the sins of the world." The angels asked, "Has the whole world heard of You?" Christ responded, "No, not yet." They wondered, "What, then, is Your plan?" Jesus explained, "I left twelve men and some other followers to carry the message to the whole world." The angels then asked, "If that doesn't work, what is plan B?" Jesus responded, "There is no plan B."

There is no other plan. God's plan is for people to reach people.

While in California, I spoke to a man named David who participated in God's plan of reaching people. When I spoke at a men's conference he attended, he told me of his father-in-law, Bob, coming to Christ through our "May I Ask You a Question?" tract (see Appendix). When he first shared the little blue tract with Bob, David didn't realize its impact. He didn't even know if Bob was that impressed. One day, months later, Bob got into his son-in-law's car and saw a "May I Ask You a Question?" tract that had slid to the floor of the car. Bob picked it up and read aloud, "Has anyone ever taken a Bible and shown you how you can know for sure you are going to heaven?" Smiling at his son-in-law across the car console, Bob said, "Yes, my son-in-law did that." It turned out that Bob had trusted Christ some time after their talk. He now knew for certain that he was going to heaven. David went home and told his wife that her dad had trusted Christ, and with tears running down her cheeks, she rejoiced with her husband. Several months later, Bob died.

It is irrefutable that God is sovereign. It is also irrefutable that He has predetermined both the end and the means. But to use the sovereignty of God as an excuse for not evangelizing is wrong. One more matter must be stressed.

Those with a biblical perspective on eternity *want* to reach the lost.

The Bible encourages us to live our lives from heaven backward. Imagine standing before the Savior. At that moment, what will be the most important thing in your life? Make that the most important thing now. If you do, when you stand before Christ, you will have no regret.

From an eternal perspective, people are what matter. Those with a biblical perspective on evangelism want to reach the lost. They want to live for what counts. They are pleased that God wants to use them to populate heaven. Instead of saying, "He doesn't need my help," they say, "I'm sure glad He wants my help."

Sandy is a delightful young woman who worked at our office for several years. As she worked with us, I saw growth in both her concern for the lost as well as her desire to reach them. One evening, riding home on the bus, a man saw her reading a book about spiritual things. He asked, "Are you a Christian?" She said, "Yes, why?" He said, "You know what really bothers me about Christians?" Sandy is shy by nature, and I can only imagine how her heart started to thud, fearful of what the man might say. She took a deep breath and asked, "What's that?" He said, "They never tell you how to get to heaven." She then said, "I'll explain it to you," and took a Bible and led him to Christ. She wanted to reach the lost and God used her to do so. God sovereignly placed Sandy and that man together on the bus. Sandy chose to respond in obedience and share the truth of God's plan of salvation.

Lewis Sperry Chafer, founder of Dallas Theological Seminary, wrote about prayer related to evangelism in his book, *True Evangelism*. He said, "Thus in the Scriptures and in experience it is revealed that God has honored man with an exalted place of cooperation and partnership with Himself in His great projects of human transformation."[1]

Conclusion

The teaching that says, "Since God is sovereign and will save whomever He chooses, He doesn't need our help," is a misconception. Being sovereign, God has predetermined the end, a truth that brings us comfort in evangelism. The results are in His hands. But He has also predetermined the means—people reaching people. To neglect one's responsibility in evangelism is to neglect a God-given responsibility. God wants the lost to come to Christ. He has predetermined that as His disciples we will be the means through which He reaches them.

> **God is sovereign. His elect will come to Him. He has also determined how they will be reached— through His people.**

"To reach a cultist, you have to know what the cult believes."

((•))

"My daughter married a Seventh Day Adventist. Can you explain what they believe so I'll know how to talk to him about Christ?"

"I'm witnessing to a Mormon who keeps bringing up the Book of Mormon. Where can I get a copy so I can read it before I talk to her?"

"What book would you recommend on Jehovah's Witnesses? I'm trying to talk to one. I need to know what they believe."

"Ever since September 11, I've been aware that I don't know what Muslims believe. Maybe I should take a class that explains the Muslim faith so I'll be more effective with them."

You've probably heard these kinds of comments. They express, "To reach a cultist, you have to know what the cult believes."

Why is that a misconception? Prior to addressing that issue, two questions need to be answered.

What is a cult?

A cult is any group of people or system of belief that does not adhere to the central doctrines of Christianity. A cult promotes a founder, a leader, and a way of eternal salvation other than the Person of Jesus Christ.

With that definition in mind, it's helpful to know what characterizes most cults. Cults err in that:

- They teach that one is saved on the basis of human merit or good works. Scriptures teach that salvation is free (Eph. 2:8–9).
- They deny the certainty of salvation. Scriptures teach that upon trusting Jesus Christ as the only way to heaven, one can be certain of salvation (1 John 5:13).
- Their self-appointed leader is the messiah. Scripture teaches that Christ alone is the Messiah (John 4:25–26).
- They deny the inspiration of Scripture, insisting there is additional revelation outside the Bible. Scripture teaches that the Word of God is inspired (meaning God-breathed) and without error (2 Tim. 3:14–16; 2 Peter 1:20–21).
- Some cults believe God is still giving additional revelation. Scripture affirms that all revelation has already been given through His Son (Heb. 1:2).
- They deny the deity of Jesus Christ. Scripture teaches that Jesus Christ was the One He claimed to be—God in the flesh (John 14:7; 20:24–29).
- They lead people into a lifestyle of bondage. Scriptures teach there is freedom in Christ (John 8:36; 10:10). We are not to be "entangled again with a yoke of bondage"(Gal. 5:1).

Is it wrong to invite a cultist into your home?

On the basis of 2 John 10–11, some wonder, "Is it a violation of Scripture to have a cultist in your home?" We read, "If anyone comes to you and does not bring this doctrine, do not receive him into your house nor greet him; for he who greets him shares in his evil deeds."

In John's day, traveling speakers were common; Hyatts and Holiday Inns were not. Therefore, a traveling speaker continuing his itinerant ministry needed help in two ways—food and lodging. We refer to that kind of hospitality as "bed and breakfast," complete with down comforter and hazelnut coffee. Should one offer such hospitality to such teachers it would encourage them in their ministry. It would say, "Let me help you as you spread your false doctrine." John forbids us to do that and says not to even greet that person. Greetings similar to "I am glad to see you" or "I wish you well" were not to be extended.

When a cultist visits your home today and you invite that person in, it's not the same situation. You're not offering that person a bed or a meal. The application, though, is, "Don't offer hospitality and encouragement." If you do what, in fact, you ought—put before cultists the clear message of the gospel of grace—their time in your home should discourage more than encourage them. But in light of the context of 2 John, moments of conversation spent in your living room presenting a cultist with that person's need for Christ is not in violation of Scripture.

Let's now turn to the misconception at hand. To reach a cultist, why does a believer *not* have to know what that cult believes?

A believer must know what Scripture teaches, not what the person in error believes.

In Ephesians 4:11–14, Paul explained one purpose for God giving spiritual gifts to people in the church: "We should no longer be children, tossed to and fro and carried about with every wind of doctrine, by the trickery of men, in the cunning craftiness of deceitful plotting."

As maturing believers, learning the Word from gifted people prevents us from being spiritually immature infants who are easily swayed and confused, tossed back and forth by every gust-of-wind teaching. Those gusts are produced by people who, with deceit, attempt to move others toward a system of error.

We need to know what the Scriptures teach, not what those in error espouse. When the FBI trains in how to detect counterfeit money, they have trainees study the authentic bill so carefully that they can recognize the counterfeit, not vice versa. In a similar way, we need to know what the Scriptures teach so that we can then recognize those in error.

When a cultist is at your door, that person is there to deliver a spiritual message. But those in error have no message for you; you have a message for them. I met a Mormon and engaged him in conversation. After turning the conversation to spiritual things, I gave him an evangelistic tract, explaining its message. He was shocked that I gave him something to read. It's usually the opposite—they give us their material. He didn't have news I needed to hear. I had news he needed to hear.

God uses the truth of the gospel to convict.

Paul reminds us of something in 2 Corinthians 4. He states that unlike his opponents, he did not distort the Word of God. He then reminds the Corinthians,

> But even if our gospel is veiled, it is veiled to those who are perishing, whose minds the god of this age has blinded, who do not believe, lest the light of the gospel of the glory of Christ, who is the image of God, should shine on them. For we do not preach ourselves, but Christ Jesus the Lord, and ourselves your bondservants for Jesus' sake. (vv. 3–5)

Why are some unwilling to accept the gospel? Their unbelief has been aided by the god of this age—Satan and his evil influences. He has so blinded minds that without the Holy Spirit it's impossible for people to understand the gospel.

So what did Paul present to those blinded by Satan? Paul focused on Christ, who is the image of God. Christ and His truth, not deceivers and their error, was the focus of his message. And as Christ is preached, the Holy Spirit convicts the lost of their need for Him. In John 16:8, the apostle explains the convicting ministry of the Holy Spirit: "And when He has come, He will convict the world of sin, and of righteousness, and of judgment." The believer should, then, so lay the truth before the lost that the truth, anointed by the Holy Spirit, can bring the lost to Christ.

Another passage where Paul affirms that God uses the message of the Cross to convict is 1 Corinthians 1:21, 23: "For since, in the wisdom of God, the world through wisdom did not know God, it pleased God through the foolishness of the message preached to save those who believe. . . . but we preach Christ crucified, to the Jews a stumbling block and to the Greeks foolishness." The Jews thought that Christ would bring in a political kingdom and they would be the administrators. Greeks, seeking after wisdom, emphasized philosophy. But God gave them the message of the Cross, the message of a crucified Christ. Through the Cross, God revealed the foolishness of men at its worst and the wisdom of God at its best. God offered what logic and debate couldn't—how to redeem the world through a crucified Christ. God uses the message of the Cross to convict, and Scripture exhorts us to keep that message simple and clear.

The believer ought to take the offensive, not the defensive.

Paul's ministry in Athens is a study in how to reach those in error. That city had more gods than people. What stood out to the unbelievers concerning Paul's approach to them? Acts 17:18 tells us, "Then certain Epicurean and Stoic philosophers encountered him. And some said, 'What does this babbler want to say?' Others said, 'He seems to be a proclaimer of foreign gods,' because he preached to them Jesus and the resurrection." They were struck by his preaching Jesus and the Resurrection.

Epicureans were atheists who believed pleasure was the only good and pain the only evil. Convinced there was no life beyond the present or future judgment, their philosophy was, "Eat, drink, and be merry." Stoics saw no distinction between the human and the divine; God was everything and everything was God. So what was Paul's approach? We are told that Paul "preached to them Jesus and the resurrection." Recognizing that what he said was something they'd never heard before, they brought him to the Aeropagus, where the latest ideas were discussed. What did they request? "May we know what this new doctrine is of which you speak?" (v. 19).

His approach was offensive, not defensive. He knew he didn't need to understand their message; they needed to understand his. It's true that many people in cults today have no idea what their own cult teaches. Rather, they joined the cult for a sense of belonging. Everyone wants to feel accepted, and cults specialize in offering acceptance, deceptive as it is.

So Paul's model for approaching those in error is still effective today. We need not defend the Christian faith, but lay out the truth of the gospel.

Makes sense, doesn't it?

The fact that one has to know what one believes, not what the cultist believes, adds up to two words—common sense. If we approach evangelism thinking that we have to know what the cultist believes in order to witness to that person, three questions emerge:

1. *Who do we prepare to talk to?* Is the next cultist you meet going to be a Mormon, Jehovah's Witness, Christian Scientist, Muslim, Hindu, Buddhist, or one of the many cults springing out of the New Age philosophies?

2. *How do you keep up?* The longer we await the Lord's return, the more departure there will be from truth. Scripture prophesies, "For the time will come when they will not endure sound doctrine, but according to their own desires, because they have itching ears, they will heap up for themselves teachers; and they will turn their ears away from the truth, and be turned aside to fables" (2 Tim. 4:3–4). There's no way to keep sufficiently informed of every new cult.

3. *How would you prepare for the exceptions?* By exceptions I mean the person who is in a cult but doesn't believe what that false religion believes. I once talked with a man who was of the Hindu faith. He made it clear that he doesn't believe what Hindus believe. Instead he believed that after death you have one more chance and that's it. He then added, "I might be wrong, but I want to believe what I want to believe." These exceptions are more normal than one might expect.

Here's one word of caution.

This doesn't mean that those who evangelize are not helped by knowing what cults believe. Biblically, though, it's not essential to know what cultists believe to reach them. Many believers have confessed, in fact, to educating cultists on the false doctrine of their cults yet not telling them of God's simple plan of salvation.

Conclusion

The idea that to reach a cultist you have to know what a cultist believes is not taught in Scripture. Believers should so know the truth of Scripture that when they hear error they recognize it. We should so present the truth of the gospel before the cultist that the truth, anointed by the Holy Spirit, can bring that person to Christ.

> **To reach cultists, believers must know what they themselves believe, not what the cult believes. God brings cultists across your path for you to explain the gospel to them, not for them to explain error to you.**

"If you're not willing to confess Me publicly, you can't be saved."

$((\bullet))$

Sarah's prayers had been wonderfully answered. After decades of praying for her wayward, drug-addicted son, Sarah led that son to Christ. Refusing the gospel many times before and wanting to go his own way, he saw no need of Christ. Finally, he came to the end of himself, realizing the One he had rejected was the One he needed. As his mother once again explained the gospel, he trusted Christ. So grateful that the Savior was now *his* Savior, he called family members and told them what happened. Without shame, he told them that he now belonged to Christ.

Few things are more enjoyable than seeing new believers tell others of their salvation. But is such a public confession of Christ a requirement of salvation? Some not only say *yes,* but use public confession as a basis for the altar call, saying that to be saved you must walk forward. One preacher said, "There are two requirements for being saved. One is to come to Christ. The other is to walk the aisle." Another, implying that, in order to be saved, one must publicly profess Christ, has said, "Whenever Christ called people He called them publicly."

Although important, a public profession of Christ, whether to a few people or walking forward in a church service, is not a scriptural requirement for salvation. Understanding where a public profession fits underscores the simplicity of the gospel as well as the importance of discipleship.

There are three immediate considerations.

In determining the place of public profession as it relates to salvation, we face three biblical considerations.

The first is John 12:42–43. The miracles of Christ were designed to wave a flag before the Jewish people, proclaiming Christ was God. Many refused to believe. John tells us, "But although He had done so many signs before them, they did not believe in Him" (v. 37). Some, though, did believe. John 12:42–43 says, "Nevertheless even among the rulers many believed in Him, but because of the Pharisees they did not confess Him, lest they should be put out of the synagogue; for they loved the praise of men more than the praise of God."

In the book of John, The words *believe in* are used consistently for saving faith. John 3:16 reads, "For God so loved the world that He gave His only begotten Son, that whoever *believes in* Him should not perish but have everlasting life" (emphasis added). John 12 points to Jewish rulers who had trusted in Christ as the Messiah, who could save them from their sin. But to confess Him publicly would have meant excommunication from the synagogue. That threat kept them from making a public confession. Yet John says they had "believed in" Christ.

A second consideration are the many verses that condition salvation upon faith alone apart from any public confession. Here are ten of the most familiar passages.

But as many as received Him, to them He gave the right to become children of God, to those who believe in His name. (John 1:12)

He who believes in Him is not condemned; but he who does not believe is condemned already, because he has not believed in the name of the only begotten Son of God. (John 3:18)

Most assuredly, I say to you, he who hears My word and believes in Him who sent Me has everlasting life, and shall not come into judgment, but has passed from death into life. (John 5:24)

Jesus said to her, "I am the resurrection and the life. He who believes in Me, though he may die, he shall live. And whoever lives and believes in Me shall never die. Do you believe this?" (John 11:25–26)

But to him who does not work but believes on Him who justifies the ungodly, his faith is accounted for righteousness. (Romans 4:5)

Therefore, having been justified by faith, we have peace with God through our Lord Jesus Christ. (Romans 5:1)

For you are all sons of God through faith in Christ Jesus. (Galatians 3:26)

For by grace you have been saved through faith, and that not of yourselves; it is the gift of God, not of works, lest anyone should boast. (Ephesians 2:8–9)

And be found in Him, not having my own righteousness, which is from the law, but that which is through faith in Christ, the righteousness which is from God by faith. (Philippians 3:9)

And this is the testimony: that God has given us eternal life, and this life is in His Son. He who has the Son has life; he who does not have the Son of God does not have life. These things I have written to you who believe in the name of the Son of God, that you may know that you have eternal life. (1 John 5:11–13)

Scripture doesn't contradict itself, and abundant references condition salvation on faith alone. Whatever place confession does have, a public confession of Christ is not a requirement for salvation.

A third consideration is the conversion of the thief on the cross.

The thieves crucified with Christ were divided in their view of Him. While one extended a condition, "If you are the Christ, save Yourself and us" (Luke 23:39); the other placed his faith in Him. He asked, "Lord, remember me when You come into Your kingdom" (v. 42). Christ's response was the best news a dying man can hear: "Assuredly, I say to you, today you will be with Me in Paradise" (v. 43).

Did he publicly tell others of his decision? There was neither time nor opportunity. It's difficult, after all, to tell others of your salvation when nailed to a cross. If confession were a requirement for salvation, either the thief was not saved, as Christ proclaimed him to be, or there are two "gospels"—one gospel or means of salvation for a person who has time to confess and the other for a person who doesn't.

What verses are used to support such a public confession?

Three passages are used to support the thought that if one is not willing to confess Christ publicly, one cannot be saved.

Romans 10:9–10

Romans 10:9–10 reads, "That if you confess with your mouth the Lord Jesus and believe in your heart that God has raised Him from the dead, you will be saved. For with the heart one believes unto righteousness, and with the mouth confession is made unto salvation." (For further treatment of this passage, the reader is directed to the author's book *Free and Clear,* Kregel Publications, 1997.) Let's consider three observations.

Here, the word *saved* refers to deliverance. Paul wrote of being saved from a shipwreck (Acts 27:20), James wrote of being saved from physical death (James 5:15), and Paul spoke of women being saved in childbearing (1 Tim. 2:15). The word *saved* doesn't always refer to eternal salvation. The context determines what one is delivered from.

At this point in the book of Romans, Paul is explaining how to be saved from the wrath of God, a theme he began in Romans 5: "Much more then, having now been justified by His blood, we shall be saved from wrath through Him. For if when we were enemies we were reconciled to God through the death of His Son, much more, having been reconciled, we shall be saved by His life" (vv. 9–10).

In order to escape God's judgment on sin, we must be justified. The word *righteousness* in Romans 10:10 is the noun form of the verb translated "justify" in passages such as Romans 5:1: "Therefore, having been justified by faith, we have peace with God through our Lord Jesus Christ." *Justified* here means to be declared righteous. The moment we come to God as sinners recognizing Jesus Christ died in our place and rose again, and trust in Christ alone to save us, a divine transaction takes place. God takes His Son's righteousness and places it in our account, and we are forever declared right with God. Therefore, the meaning of this first part of verse 10 is, "With the heart man believes and is justified before God."

To escape God's wrath on present sin, though, we must also confess Christ publicly. Paul continues in Romans 10:10: "And with the mouth confession is made unto salvation." One becomes a Christian simply by trusting Christ. That is the only way to become a Christian—trusting Christ alone as our only basis for right standing with God. But one cannot be a victorious Christian and experience deliverance from present day sin without openly declaring one's faith. Paul continues in verses 11–13, "For the Scripture says, 'Whoever believes on Him will not be put to shame.' For there is no distinction between Jew and Greek, for the same Lord over all is rich to all who call upon Him. For 'whoever calls on the name of the LORD shall be saved.'" The person who trusts Christ will not be disappointed. Therefore, there's no need to be embarrassed about making such a confession. Should one need the assistance of God to make that confession, one is encouraged to "call upon the name of the Lord"—a phrase used in Scripture for worshiping Him and asking for His assistance (cf. Joel 2:32). Before such a call can be made, though, one has to believe. Hence Paul continues, "How then shall they call on Him in whom they have not believed? And how shall they believe in Him of whom they have not heard? And how shall they hear without a preacher?" (v. 14).

Romans 10:9–10, then, does not teach that confession is a requirement for salvation from eternal damnation. It teaches that a confession is necessary to live a victorious Christian life.

One night, Tammy and I discovered a leak in our roof. The discolored ceiling and musty smell were clues. So Tammy contacted a roofer. He was one of those friendly, trustworthy types whose broad Texas smile was as genuine as his work. As they talked, Tammy turned the conversation to spiritual things. After he left, she wrote to him and enclosed one of our tracts that explained that salvation was not through Christ plus, but Christ alone. That tract so touched him that he called and told her how much it meant to him. Now that he was certain of his salvation, Tammy stressed that eternal life was a gift.

A year later, a hailstorm pummeled our area. The dents in the shingles, visible from the yard, affirmed the roof had to be replaced, so we hired the same roofer. He came to pick up my check one evening when Tammy wasn't at home. His beaming eyes, friendly smile, and relaxed posture on the chair told me he wanted to sit and talk. I also guessed he had something to share. He said, "I keep that letter and tract your wife gave me inside my Bible. I read it every Sunday when I go to church." He said that three times as he explained how much it meant to know that he was saved through Christ alone. We aren't sure if he trusted Christ through Tammy's interaction or if he came to know Christ as a child and then forgot the simplicity of the message. He assured me, though, that he now understood that Christ alone saves.

As someone who now understood the gospel, he was vocal about his faith and unashamed to tell others. It was obvious that his public profession of Christ affected his victorious walk. As one trying to walk in the footsteps of Christ, his work and witness were being used by God.

Matthew 10:32–33

In Matthew 10:32–33 Christ declares, "Therefore whoever confesses Me before men, him I will also confess before My Father who is in heaven. But whoever denies Me before men, him I will also deny before

My Father who is in heaven." Emphasizing "whoever denies Me before men, him I will also deny before My Father," some conclude a public confession of Christ is essential to salvation.

The context removes any question that confession is required for eternal life. The context is discipleship. Several verses earlier we read, "A disciple is not above his teacher, nor a servant above his master. It is enough for a disciple that he be like his teacher, and a servant like his master. If they have called the master of the house Beelzebub, how much more will they call those of his household!" (vv. 24–25).

How would his disciples be affected for denying Him out of fear of persecution and possibly death (v. 28)? It would not change their salvation, but it would affect their eternal reward. Several verses later, continuing His theme of discipleship, Christ explains, "He who receives a prophet in the name of a prophet shall receive a prophet's reward. And he who receives a righteous man in the name of a righteous man shall receive a righteous man's reward. And whoever gives one of these little ones only a cup of cold water in the name of a disciple, assuredly, I say to you, he shall by no means lose his reward" (vv. 41–42). All saved people get to heaven, but all saved people are not equally rewarded. People who trust Christ but do not confess Him will not lose their salvation but their eternal reward will be affected.

Christ's warning, "Whoever denies Me before men, him I will also deny before My Father," did not put their salvation at stake. He warned the disciples of the danger of losing reward in heaven. Should we deny Him, when we stand before Him for reward, He will deny that we have been faithful disciples.

2 Timothy 2:11–13

In 2 Timothy 2:11–13 Paul exhorts, "This is a faithful saying: For if we died with Him, we shall also live with Him. If we endure, we shall also reign with Him. If we deny Him, He also will deny us. If we are faithless, He remains faithful; He cannot deny Himself." Doesn't that imply we must publicly profess Christ to be saved?

Paul referred to hardships such as those mentioned in verse 10 when he said, "I endure all things for the sake of the elect." Those who endure are promised reward in heaven. They shall "reign with Him." To reign is spoken of as reward in passages such as Revelation 3:21: "To him who overcomes I will grant to sit with Me on My throne, as I also overcame and sat down with My Father on His throne."

What about those who deny Him? Even when we are faithless, He cannot deny Himself. We might break our promise to Him, but He cannot break His promise to us. He is faithful. What Paul meant by "faithless" as connected with denial is not certain. But even when we are faithless toward Him, He remains faithful to us. He never takes back the salvation that was given at the moment we trusted Christ. Instead, as Romans 11:29 promises, "The gifts and the calling of God are irrevocable." We may walk away from Him, but He never walks away from us.

Conclusion

A public confession of Christ is of eternal importance. But its importance is not related to our eternal salvation. It relates to our victorious Christian life now and ultimately to our eternal reward. Upon trusting Christ we receive His gift of eternal life; upon confessing Christ consistently and unashamedly, we experience victory over sin and gain eternal reward when we see the Savior face to face.

> **A public profession of Christ is not a requirement for receiving eternal life. Confession relates to discipleship and reward. To be saved, there is but one requirement—"Believe on the Lord Jesus Christ."**

"You shouldn't witness until your life is all it should be. You could do more harm than good."

((•))

Life has turned upside down for your neighbors. After years of everything going right, now everything is going wrong. The wife was burned in a near-fatal car accident and, although fortunate to be alive, she'll bear scars the rest of her life. The husband has an engineering job—for a year. The company he works for plans to downsize, and no doubt he'll be let go. Then last week he got a call that his brother in Minnesota has been diagnosed with advanced colon cancer. All this during a time when their sixteen-year-old daughter is dating someone of whom they disapprove.

Problems drive some people away from God, but this family seems to be moving closer to God. Until recently they were unapproachable about spiritual things, but it now appears that the door of opportunity has opened a crack.

So why don't you talk to them? What holds you back? Could it be that the neighbors know a few details about your life? One evening, for example, when your mower wouldn't start, you spoke loudly of the Lord—but not the way a Christian ought to use His name. Nor did the backyard fence prevent the neighbors from hearing the bitter argument you and your wife had. Weren't you embarrassed to find out they were sunbathing in their backyard and heard every word? Instead of reflecting Christians who seem to have it all together, your conduct and conversation might lead them to believe it's all falling apart. "If I mention Christ," you wonder, "what will they think? How can I talk of the Lord when my life isn't what it should be? Won't I do more harm than good?"

Some say, "You shouldn't witness until your life is all it should be." While the danger of hindering instead of helping the cause of Christ is real, such a thought is a misconception. Why?

We must not be victims of extremes.

Yes, life is important to witness. That was addressed when we dealt with the misconception, "Living a Christlike life around non-Christians is enough. You really don't need to use words."

Peter said, "Beloved, I beg you as sojourners and pilgrims, abstain from fleshly lusts which war against the soul, having your conduct honorable among the Gentiles, that when they speak against you as evildoers, they may, by your good works which they observe, glorify God in the day of visitation" (1 Peter 2:11–12).

Peter urged believers to live apart from the immorality and sinful desires surrounding them. Why? It was important to their spiritual well-being. It was also important to maintaining an effective witness before unbelievers. Peter used the word *honorable* to refer to their character and *good* to refer to their works. Both come from the same Greek word that refers to goodness of character and deeds. Such behavior glorifies God before those who slander or accuse us. Christ, in fact, used goodness to win others to Him. "In the day of visitation" may refer to the final judgment when every tongue will confess that He is God (Phil. 2:11). It more likely refers to the day that God brings nonbelievers to saving faith in Christ. As He deals with non-Christians, God uses goodness of character and deeds in a believer to point nonbelievers to His Son. So our lives are, indeed, important to our witness.

The devotional *Our Daily Bread* once told of a man who entered a maximum security prison to minister to inmates. He was told that his identification card had been misplaced. The guard had to fill out a temporary permission slip to allow him to enter and teach his Bible class. After he showed his driver's license, the guard completed the form to let him in. As the believer glanced at it, he noticed a space for the name of the person he was representing. The guard had written in bold, black letters, "God."[1] As believers we represent God. So our lives are important to our witness.

But we need to avoid the other extreme. Danger lies there as well.

If you wait until your life is everything it should be, you'll never evangelize.

I spoke at a church where a woman professed that she had reached sinless perfection. Not only did she not sin, she said that she'd come to a point where she felt she couldn't sin. After I spoke on the characteristics of love (1 Cor. 13), the woman saw me after church. She said, "Thanks for your message. I took notes for my son [who was not there]. He really needs this." As she walked out the door, she turned and said, "I suppose I could use it too."

On any given day, who, if we were honest, could say, "My life is one hundred percent for Christ, as it should be"? If we say that, we've already sinned—a sin called pride. More often, we would agree with Paul: "For the good that I will to do, I do not do; but the evil I will not to do, that I practice" (Rom. 7:19). True humility forces us to exclaim, "O wretched man that I am!" (v. 24). God does not save perfect people. God saves sinners—sinners who will not be sinless until they see the Savior face to face.

If you wait until your life is all it should be, you'll never evangelize. Satan knows that, and being the master of intimidation, he uses that misconception to discourage us in evangelism. He understands that there would never be a day you'd be free to evangelize.

Non-Christians do not expect perfection; they expect honesty about our failures.

I've never met one unbeliever who expected Christians to be perfect. They know that Christians are human, that they will fail. Unbelievers don't expect perfection, but they do expect integrity. It's one thing to fail; it's another thing to come across as someone who never does. When we fail, whether with an unkind act or an unkind word, the words *I'm sorry* should jump freely from our tongues. People who are winsome know how to apologize.

Testimonies are exciting. I love to hear how people come to the Savior. So I often ask believers, "How did you come to know the Lord?" I'll never forget one response. A man I'll call Carl told me about a neighbor who had a noticeable character flaw and often offended others. Carl also mentioned that the neighbor was evangelistic, and not long after meeting Carl, the neighbor witnessed to him. Carl then said, "He was transparent about his failures and even addressed the one that bothered me. That honesty made me want to listen. He led me to the Savior, but I don't think I would've listened to him if he hadn't been honest about his failures." In more than thirty years of evangelism, I've never met a non-Christian who expected perfection of believers. They do, though, want us to be honest.

Confession of sin takes seconds, not years.

When evangelizing, we pray for opportunities, boldness, open doors, and the salvation of lost people. But the psalmist says, "If I regard iniquity in my heart, the Lord will not hear" (Ps. 66:18). The idea in this psalm is not only sinning but clinging to sin. The psalmist calls upon nations everywhere to praise the Lord for His deliverance of Israel. Had the psalmist clung to sin, God wouldn't have answered his prayer for deliverance. Sin causes God to turn His face from us (Isa. 59:2), because sin is repugnant to God. Clinging to sin prevents our prayers from being answered.

How long does it take to cleanse one's heart before God? Seconds. The moment we do, 1 John 1:9 tells us, "He is faithful and just to forgive us our sins and to cleanse us from all unrighteousness."

As we have opportunities to share the gospel, God hears the whispers of our hearts. With sincerity, we can ask God to forgive our bitter tongues. We can admit lustfulness and ask forgiveness. We can ask for God's forgiveness for impatience with our mates and children. The moment we confess is the moment we experience His kind, gracious, and eternal forgiveness. We are a cleansed vessel fit for His use.

God uses imperfect people.

Examine in Scripture the people whom God used. They weren't perfect examples of godliness. At best, they were imperfect people serving a perfect God. Consider David, for example. Scripture calls David a man after God's own heart (1 Sam. 13:14). He's considered by some as the greatest king Israel ever had. A hunger for God and His righteousness permeated David's life. His accomplishments as king, warrior, musician, and prophet would fill volumes. When he neared the end of his life, what did he hand to his son Solomon? A unified nation, a military force respected by all enemies, Israel's boundaries having been extended from six thousand to sixty thousand square miles, and extensive trade routes having been established. Yet his record is stained by two of the grossest sins one could commit. He committed adultery, and to cover up his sin he murdered the husband of the woman with whom he had the affair. Yet God did not apologize for having used him, nor did it prevent God, once David repented, from using him further. First Chronicles 29:28 contains his epitaph: "So he died in a good old age, full of days and riches and honor; and Solomon his son reigned in his place."

Samson is also listed in the Faith Hall of Fame (Heb. 11:32). What he did through God's strength is amazing. He killed a lion, thirty Philistines, and one thousand men with his bare hands. He ripped the cords used to bind him and carried off the gates of Gaza. Yet he could be carnal, childish, and full of sexual lust. Still, wanting to be used of God, even at the cost of his own life, he literally pulled down the temple of Dagon. The punishment on the evil worshipers was such that "the dead that he killed at his death were more than he had killed in his life" (Judg. 16:30).

Turn to the New Testament. Who failed Christ at a most critical hour? Peter. Peter had walked at the side of Jesus, and had learned at His feet, yet three times Peter denied the Savior. Still, God used him as a leader in the early church, and through his witness to Cornelius took the gospel to the Gentiles. His evangelistic preaching impacted many.

God uses imperfect people. The issue, then, is not our sinfulness. Rather, it's our willingness to repent and be used by God.

God works through us and, at times, in spite of us.

God desires God-honoring thoughts, attitudes, and actions as we evangelize. But even when our lives and our motives are not what they should be, God can still be glorified.

Throughout his ministry, Paul was determined to go to Rome to evangelize the city. After his third missionary journey, he was arrested in Jerusalem, taken to Caesarea, and finally to Rome as a prisoner. In his final three years he experienced imprisonment, rejection, and a conspiracy to kill him.

Did Rome hear the gospel? Yes. Guards who were chained to Paul heard the gospel through his own voice and carried that message back to the barracks. How else did Rome hear? Paul explained, "And most of the brethren in the Lord, having become confident by my chains, are much more bold to speak the word without fear" (Phil. 1:14). Paul's courage inspired others. Did they all preach Christ with the right motive? Paul continued, "Some indeed preach Christ even from envy and strife, and some also from goodwill: the former preach Christ from selfish ambition, not sincerely, supposing to add affliction to my chains; but the latter out of love, knowing that I am appointed for the defense of the gospel" (vv. 15–17).

Some preached Christ out of love for the Lord and the lost; others did it out of love for themselves. With Paul off the scene, they grabbed the spotlight, and adding to Paul's misery enticed them further. As spiritually sick as their motives were, Paul's comfort was that they were preaching Christ. He condoned their message, not their motives. God worked through them and also in spite of them.

A certain Bible college had a tremendous reputation for its clarity with the gospel. Satan, being the evil one he is, tempted the president into an adulterous relationship. The touch of another woman's hand meant more than the touch of his wife's. He eventually left his wife for the other woman, and both the students and the college suffered. Their testimony was reduced to zero and the college folded. Did God use this man to impact others with the gospel even while he was living in sin? Yes. Not only did he motivate and train students, he even led others to Christ during the period of sinfulness. God worked through his life even though it was dishonoring to Him.

A pastor whose friendship meant a lot to me was a devoted follower of Christ. God used him greatly to plan an outreach where I spoke. Many non-Christians attended and trusted Christ. I went on to have several outreaches with him, all of which produced spiritual fruit. Sad to say, Satan also tempted him to immorality. He gave in to temptation and became sexually involved with a woman in the church. He left his wife, and she, their family, and the testimony of the church in that community suffered. Nothing, though, negates the fact that, even while he was living in sin, God worked in spite of it.

What God *prefers* to use and what He *can* use are not always the same. God desires to use a clean instrument, but there are times when, in His grace, He works in spite of us.

Conclusion

While a godly life enhances one's witness, we mustn't be extreme in thinking that unless our lives are all they should be we shouldn't share the Good News. If we had to be near perfect to evangelize, no witnessing would ever occur. Unbelievers expect us to be honest about our mistakes; they don't expect us never to make them. A heart that is not right with God can be cleansed immediately upon confession of sinfulness. God delights in using sinners who are saved by grace.

> **Our witness could be damaged by our lives. But waiting to evangelize until our lives are all they should be is a ploy of Satan. God uses us in spite of our imperfections.**

"I'm disappointed with your results in evangelism. You haven't led many people to Me."

((•))

Tomorrow at 3:00 P.M. is your annual review. Sweat pops out on your forehead. Will you be able to sleep tonight? What's your boss going to say? Is he pleased or disappointed? There's reason for concern. Your first year hasn't been as productive as he expected. You think, *I wish I were giving the evaluation, instead of the one being evaluated.*

What does a boss look for in an employee? Results. Employees have to be worth their salaries. Otherwise, the people on the payroll cost more than they produce. Stated or unstated, the employer is saying, "I want to see results."

Many think that God says the same thing about evangelism. The number of people whom we share Christ with doesn't matter because we think that God expects us to *lead* others to Him, not just *tell* about Him.

As a result, several things happen. Our approach becomes more high pressure. It doesn't matter whether non-Christians come to Christ of their own will or ours, just as long as they make the list. We can't afford the wasted time of sharing the gospel if we don't see a response. We think that God is keeping records. We need a *yes* from the lost, so we pressure and manipulate to get it. The problem is, that's not a Holy Spirit produced convert. It's a human spirit produced one, which is no convert at all.

The second thing that happens is we get discouraged. If we have few results, we think we haven't merited anything with God, so why keep trying? We're doomed to fail in evangelism, we think we're a disappointment to God, and we fear seeing Him face to face.

What's the error in this thinking? Why is it a misconception?

No verse teaches that God holds us responsible for winning the lost.

Where do we get the idea that we're responsible for *winning* the lost? No such verse exists. Nor is there a hint that when we stand before God to be rewarded, He will ask, "How many have you led to Me?" He wouldn't have to ask such a question—He already knows.

But what about 1 Corinthians 9:19–23?

> For though I am free from all men, I have made myself a servant to all, that I might win the more; and to the Jews I became as a Jew, that I might win Jews; to those who are under the law, as under the law, that I might win those who are under the law; to those who are without law, as without law (not being without law toward God, but under law toward Christ), that I might win those who are without law; to the weak I became as weak, that I might win the weak. I have become all things to all men, that I might by all means save some. Now this I do for the gospel's sake, that I may be partaker of it with you.

Paul uses the term *win* five times here. Closing the paragraph, he says, "That I might by all means *save* some." Wasn't it Paul's thinking that God expected him to save people, not just witness to them?

The context, though, clears up any confusion. "Those . . . under the law" refers to Jews; "those . . . without law" refers to Gentiles. Coming to Christ, Paul, as a Jew, recognized that he wasn't under the Old Testament law. He also recognized some Jews would feel scandalized if he didn't observe the law. Because he loved them, he accommodated them, observing many of their feasts and festivals. In doing so, he led Jews and Gentiles to Christ.

When Paul speaks of liberties he's willing to forfeit in order to "win the more," he's actually talking about the winning of a hearing. One commentator makes the point, "He was willing to subject himself to the scruples of the Jews in order to gain a hearing for the gospel and to win them to Christ. Yet he never compromised the essence of the gospel, at the heart of which was salvation by faith, not works and freedom from legalism."[1] *Win* and *save* refer to gaining acceptance and a hearing; nothing indicates that God held Paul responsible for the salvation of any Jew or Gentile.

Another might ask, what about Proverbs 11:30? "The fruit of the righteous is a tree of life, and he who wins souls is wise." Isn't the emphasis on winning not sharing? This verse isn't about evangelism. The phrase "fruit of the righteous" refers to the good a righteous man does for others. His words, actions, instruction, and example uplift others. Thus, the good he does is a "tree of life." The phrase "he who wins souls is wise" means that a wise man wins people to him. This can be done for sinister reasons, such as using others for selfish gain, but here it's meant in a good sense. The wise man captivates people, having a good influence upon them.

Proverbs 11:30 teaches that righteousness produces fruit, wisdom produces influence. A righteous person produces fruit that has a positive effect upon others. He then uses his influence to win people to him. Although the verse is not talking about evangelism, there could be an application. People often are drawn to Christ because a believer's life attracts them. Consequently, we ought to be "living epistles" to non-Christians. The verse, though, isn't speaking of God's expectation for us to *win* the lost.

God holds us responsible for contact, not conversion.

What did Jesus commission His disciples to do? Acts 1:8 says, "But you shall receive power when the Holy Spirit has come upon you; and you shall be witnesses to Me in Jerusalem, and in all Judea and Samaria, and to the end of the earth."

A witness tells what he or she knows. The disciples were to tell what they knew, starting at Jerusalem, the local city—the very city where Christ was rejected and crucified. They were to go from there to the local area of Judea. With Samaria mentioned and Galilee implied, this meant the outer area of Palestine. They were then to go to "the end of the earth," which to the apostles likely would have been Rome, the capital of the empire and the place where people congregated from every quarter. A direct line drawn from Judea to Rome would have been more than fourteen hundred miles long. The book of Acts records the progress of the gospel, first in Jerusalem (chaps. 1–7), then in all Judea and Samaria (chaps. 8–12), and finally to the worldwide Gentile sphere (chaps. 13–28).

The emphasis of the commission is on the disciples's responsibility to bring Christ to non-Christians, not to bring non-Christians to Christ. Proclamation was the issue, not results. Beginning at home, they were to tell what they knew unto the ends of the earth.

Personal evangelism is impossible without personal contact. That's why Christ's own example stressed the need to be a friend of sinners (Luke 15:2). We can't speak to those whom we haven't contacted. We must go to them. We must be witnesses. What results from that contact is never the issue. Rather, the biblical emphasis is contact, not conversion.

God holds us responsible for faithfulness, not fruit.

Notice Paul's response when mistreated by the Corinthians who showed partiality toward certain teachers. He said,

> Let a man so consider us, as servants of Christ and stewards of the mysteries of God. Moreover it is required in stewards that one be found faithful. But with me it is a very small thing that I should be judged by you or by a human court. In fact, I do not even judge myself. For I know of nothing against myself, yet I am not justified by this; but He who judges me is the Lord. (1 Cor. 4:1–4)

Ministers are servants of Christ. As stewards of His truth, they dispense what they are given. What is their responsibility as they dispense truth? It is as Paul explained, "That one be found faithful." He didn't say "That one be found *fruitful*." Only when we stand before the Lord will we find out how faithful we've been. No one else can make the final prognosis. Instead, Paul said, "He who judges me is the Lord."

That the Lord judges one's level of faithfulness gives meaning to Paul's words one chapter earlier when he rebuked the Corinthian's partisan spirit. He reminded them that he and Apollos were both used of the Lord in starting and growing the church:

> Who then is Paul, and who is Apollos, but ministers through whom you believed, as the Lord gave to each one? I planted, Apollos watered, but God gave the increase. So then neither he who plants is anything, nor he who waters, but God who gives the increase. Now he who plants and he who waters are one, and each one will receive his own reward according to his own labor. (1 Cor. 3:5–8)

Paul planted the church. Apollos ministered after Paul left. Both were used of the Lord. Our responsibility is to be faithful in whatever we're doing, and God rewards our labors. Fruitfulness is God's responsibility.

Consider the principle of sowing and reaping.

Why is it important to understand that faithfulness is the issue? As noted in a previous chapter, at times we will sow the seeds of the gospel, and someone else may reap the seeds we've sown. During His visit to Samaria, Christ said, "'One sows and another reaps.' I sent you to reap that for which you have not labored; others have labored, and you have entered into their labors" (John 4:37–38). Although He was only in Samaria two days and did no miracles, Christ found a field ripe unto harvest. Apparently, the ministry of the Old Testament prophets and John the Baptist had their results. Christ assured His disciples that both the sower and the reaper will have their reward.

Our office received a call from a woman in Pennsylvania. She told us that a person had just dropped one of our "May I Ask You a Question?" tracts (see Appendix) by her house. As a result of reading it, she trusted Christ. Since EvanTell's name and phone number were on the back, she wanted to know how to get more copies. She was thrilled with what she now understood and wanted others to know. I thought, *I'm certain the person who left the tract along with any others who witnessed to her don't even know what their efforts accomplished.* Her receptivity indicated that months and perhaps years earlier someone had sown the seed of the gospel. Now, it had born fruit. The "end" person may not even know what his or her efforts accomplished. Everyone who had a part in her coming to Christ will be rewarded.

Christ taught that only He could bring the lost to Himself.

The responsibility of bringing the lost to Christ is on God's shoulders. It is not on the shoulders of His servants. Jesus explains in John 6:44, "No one can come to Me unless the Father who sent Me draws him; and I will raise him up at the last day." Christ repeats that emphasis when He says, "Therefore I have said to you that no one can come to Me unless it has been granted to him by My Father" (v. 65). People are so ensnared in sin that unless God draws them, they're hopeless.

Why? Because they are blinded. Second Corinthians 4:4 described them as people "whose minds the god of this age has blinded, who do not believe, lest the light of the gospel of the glory of Christ, who is the image of God, should shine on them." God has to remove the veil from their eyes. Unless He does, it will never be removed. He may use a human instrument to do so, whether a preacher or someone witnessing one on one. Ultimately, though, it is Christ working. The instrument is only the means of removing the blindness; the instrument is not the power by which the blindness is removed. The power belongs to Him.

Clarity—that's the pressure we ought to feel.

The pressure of bringing people to Christ is God's. We can only bring Christ to people. The only pressure we ought to feel is the pressure to make the gospel clear.

As Christ hung on the cross, He declared, "It is finished" (John 19:30). Before a holy God He did everything that could be done to satisfy the anger of God against sin. His payment for our sin was complete and final. He and He alone atoned for our sins. To get to heaven, we cannot trust Christ *plus* something (such as our good deeds and religious efforts). Christ alone saves.

When we make the gospel clear, only Christ through His Holy Spirit can bring about an understanding of the gospel. But God uses the clarity of our presentation to show the unsaved their condition, His remedy, and their need to trust Christ. As you evangelize, say to yourself, "I must be clear, be clear, be clear."

Conclusion

Remember, God holds us responsible for contact, not conversion. We have the privilege of introducing the lost to Christ, but the pressure for them to trust the Savior is upon Him, not us.

As we improve our skills we increase our effectiveness in reaching the lost. But even when multitudes respond, God brings them, not us. Any pressure we should feel is that of making the gospel clear to lost people with the intent of them trusting Christ. Whether or not they do is God's responsibility.

> **God does not count our converts. He examines our faithfulness, and rewards our labors. The results are in His hands, not ours.**

Appendix

"May I Ask You a Question?" Tract

$((\bullet))$

EvanTell's "May I Ask You a Question?" tract has been helpful in introducing millions to Christ. The tract may be ordered from EvanTell, Inc., by calling the toll-free number (1-800-947-7359) or through EvanTell's online store at www.evantell.org.

Has anyone ever taken
a Bible
and shown you how
you can

KNOW

for sure that you're
going to heaven?

The Bible contains both

**bad
news**

and

**GOOD
news**

The *bad news*
is something about **YOU**.

The *good news*
is something about **GOD**.

Let's look at the
bad news first . . .

Bad News #1

You are a sinner.

Romans 3:23 says, *"For all have sinned and fall short of the glory of God."*

"Sinned" means that we have missed the mark. When we lie, hate, lust, or gossip, we have missed the standard God has set.

Suppose you and I were each to throw a rock and try to hit the North Pole.

You might throw farther than I, but neither of us would hit it.

When the Bible says, "All have sinned and fall short," it means that we have all come short of God's standard of perfection.

In thoughts, words, and deeds, we have not been perfect.

But the bad news gets worse . . .

Bad News #2

The penalty for sin is death.

Romans 6:23 says,
"For the wages of sin is death."

Suppose you worked for me and I paid you $50. That $50 was your wages. That's what you earned.

The Bible says that *by sinning we have earned death*. That means we deserve to die and be separated from God forever.

But...

since there
was no way you
could come to God,
the Bible says that God
decided to come to you.

Good News #1

Christ died for you.

Romans 5:8 tells us, *"But God demonstrates His own love toward us, in that while we were still sinners, Christ died for us."*

Suppose you are in a hospital dying of cancer. I come to you and say,

"Let's take the cancer cells from *your* body and put them into *my* body."

If that were possible,

- What would happen to me?

- What would happen to you?

I would die in your place.
I would die instead of you.

The Bible says Christ took the penalty that we deserved for sin, placed it upon Himself, and *died in our place.*

Three days later Christ came back to life to prove that sin and death had been conquered and that His claims to be God were true.

Just as the bad news got worse, the good news gets better!

Good News #2

You can be saved through faith in Christ.

Ephesians 2:8,9 says, *"For by grace [undeserved favor] you have been saved [delivered from sin's penalty] through faith, and that not of yourselves; it is the gift of God, not of works, lest anyone should boast."*

Faith means *trust.*

Question: What must you trust Christ for?

Answer: You must depend on Him alone to forgive you and to give you eternal life.

Just as you trust a chair to hold you through no effort of your own, so *you must trust Jesus Christ to get you to heaven* through no effort of your own.

But you may say,

"I'm religious."

"I'm a good person."

"I help the poor."

"I don't steal."

"I go to church."

These are all good, but good living, going to church, helping the poor, or any other good thing you might do cannot get you to heaven.

You must trust in Jesus Christ alone, and God will give you eternal life as a gift!

Does this make sense to you?

Is there anything keeping you from trusting Christ right now?

1._____

2._____

3._____

4._____

Think carefully. There is nothing more important than your need to trust Christ.

Would you like to tell God you are **trusting Jesus Christ as your Savior?**

If you would, why not pray right now and tell God you are trusting His Son?

Remember!

It is not a prayer that saves you. It is trusting Jesus Christ that saves you. Prayer is simply how you tell God what you are doing.

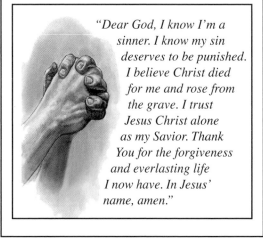

"Dear God, I know I'm a sinner. I know my sin deserves to be punished. I believe Christ died for me and rose from the grave. I trust Jesus Christ alone as my Savior. Thank You for the forgiveness and everlasting life I now have. In Jesus' name, amen."

What has just happened?

John 5:24 explains, *"He who hears My word and believes in Him who sent Me has everlasting life, and shall not come into judgment, but has passed from death into life."*

Did you "*hear*" God's word?

Did you "*believe*" what God said and trust Christ as your Savior?

Does "*has* everlasting life" mean later or right now?

Does it say "*shall not* come into judgment" or *might not*?

Does it say "*has passed* from death" or *shall pass*?

Eternal life is based on fact, not feeling.

Memorize John 5:24 today.

What do you do now?

Having trusted Christ as your only way to heaven, here's how to grow in your relationship with Him.

- *Tell God* what's on your mind through prayer (Philippians 4:6,7).

- *Read the Bible* every day (2 Timothy 3:16,17). Start in the book of Philippians.

- *Worship* with God's people in a local church (Hebrews 10:24,25).

- *Tell others* about Jesus Christ (Matthew 4:19).

If you found this booklet helpful, please share it with someone.

If you have further questions about what is contained in this booklet, contact:

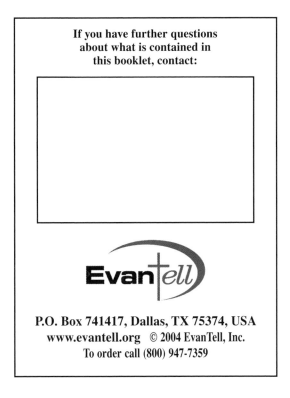

Endnotes

((•))

Misconception 10

1. Os Guinness, *In Two Minds* (Downers Grove, Ill.: Intervarsity Press, 1976), 20–21.

Misconception 11

1. Mahatma Ghandi quoted in Warren W. Wiersbe, *Be Rich* (Wheaton, Ill.: Victor Books, 1976), 97–98.

Misconception 14

1. G. A. Johnson Ross quoted in *Christian Clippings*, (October 1988): 13–14.

Misconception 16

1. Jack and Billy Campbell, "Jesus Use Me." 1956, 1963 G.P.H. Assigned 1997 to The Lorenz Corporation. All rights reserved. International copyright secured.

Misconception 17

1. Lewis Sperry Chafer, *True Evangelism* (Grand Rapids, Mich.: Dunham Publishing, 1919), 89.

Misconception 20

1. "Representing God," (December 2001).

Misconception 21

1. David K. Lowery, "1 Corinthians," in *The Bible Knowledge Commentary*, ed. John F. Walvoord and Roy B. Zuck (Wheaton, Ill.: Scripture Press Publications, Victor Books, 1983), 524.